Paper F1

Accountant in Business

EXAM KIT

British Library Cataloguing-in-Publication Data

A catalogue record for this book is available from the British Library.

Published by:
Kaplan Publishing UK
Unit 2 The Business Centre
Molly Millars Lane
Wokingham
Berkshire
RG41 2QZ

ISBN 978 1 84710 477 9

© FTC Kaplan Limited, November 2007

Printed and bound in Great Britain by William Clowes Ltd, Beccles, Suffolk

Acknowledgements

The past ACCA exam questions are the copyright of the Association of Chartered Certified Accountants. The original answers to the questions from June 1994 onwards were produced by the examiners themselves and have been adapted by Kaplan Publishing.

We are grateful to the Chartered Institute of Management Accountants and the Institute of Chartered Accountants in England and Wales for permission to reproduce past exam questions. The answers have been prepared by Kaplan Publishing.

CONTENTS

Section

INDEX TO QUESTIONS AND ANSWERS

PRACTICE QUESTIONS

SYLLABUS AND EXAM FORMAT

Format of the paper-based and computer-based exam

	Number of marks
Section A: 40 compulsory multiple-choice questions (2 marks each)	80
Section B: 10 compulsory short-form questions (1 mark each)	10
	90

Total time allowed: 2 hours

Aim

To introduce knowledge and understanding of the business and its environment and the influence this has on how organisations are structured and on the role of the accounting and other key business functions in contributing to the efficient, effective and ethical management and development of an organisation and its people and systems.

Objectives

On successful completion of this paper, candidates should be able to:

- explain how the organisation is structured, governed and managed by – and on behalf of – its external, connected and internal stakeholders

- identify and describe the key environmental influences and constraints on how the business operates in general and how these affect the accounting function in particular

- describe the history, purpose and position of accounting in the organisation, and the roles of other functional areas

- identify and explain the functions of accounting systems and internal controls in planning, monitoring and reviewing performance and in preventing fraud and business failure

- recognise the principles of authority and leadership, and how teams and individuals behave and are managed, disciplined and motivated in pursuit of wider departmental and organisational aims and objectives

- recruit and develop effective employees, using appropriate methods and procedures, while developing constructive relationships through effective communication and interpersonal skills.

Relational diagram of main capabilities

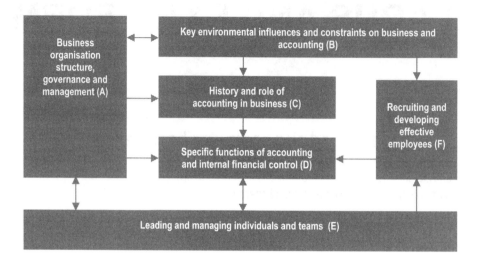

Rationale

The *Accountant in Business* syllabus acts as an introduction to business structure and purpose, and to accountancy as a central business function. The syllabus commences with an examination of the structure and governance of businesses, briefly introducing ethics. It then looks at business in the context of its environment, including economic, legal, and regulatory influences on such aspects as governance, employment, health and safety, data protection and security. From there, it focuses on accounting, how it originated, how it is organised, its critical importance in business planning and control, and how it affects other business functions.

The syllabus then introduces students to the accounting profession and to certain aspects of the regulatory framework as they affect accounting, auditing and governance. The syllabus also covers accounting, auditing, and internal control as specific business functions and how these should be supported by effective management information systems. Finally, the syllabus introduces key management and people issues such as individual and team behaviour, leadership, motivation and personal effectiveness.

Detailed Syllabus

A   Business organisation structure, governance and management

1   The business organisation and its structure

2   The formal and informal business organisation

3   Organisational culture in business

4   Stakeholders of business organisations

5   Information technology and information systems in business

6   Committees in the business organisation

7   Business ethics and ethical behaviour

8   Governance and social responsibility in business

B   Key environmental influences and constraints on business and accounting

1   Political and legal factors

2   Macro-economic factors

3   Social and demographic factors

4   Technological factors

5   Competitive factors

C   History and role of accounting in business

1   The history and function of accounting in business

2   Law and regulation governing accounting

3   Financial systems, procedures and IT applications

4   The relationship between accounting and other business functions

D   Specific functions of accounting and internal financial control

1   Accounting and finance functions within business

2   Internal and external auditing and their functions

3   Internal financial control and security within business organisations

4   Fraud and fraudulent behaviour, and their prevention in business

E   Leading and managing individuals and teams

1   Leadership, management and supervision

2   Individual and group behaviour in business organisations

3   Team formation, development and management

4   Motivating individuals and groups

F   Recruiting and developing effective employees

1   Recruitment and selection, managing diversity and equal opportunity.

2   Techniques for improving personal effectiveness at work and their benefits

3   Features of effective communication

4   Training, development, and learning in the maintenance and improvement of business performance

5   Review and appraisal of individual performance

Approach to examining the syllabus

The syllabus is assessed by a two hour paper-based or computer-based examination. Questions will assess all parts of the syllabus and will test knowledge and some comprehension or application of this knowledge. The examination will consist of 40 two mark questions, and 10 one mark questions.

Syllabus content

A BUSINESS ORGANISATIONAL STRUCTURE, GOVERNANCE AND MANAGEMENT

1 The business organisation and its structure

(a) Identify the different types of organisation: [1]

    (i) commercial

    (ii) not-for-profit

    (iii) public sector

    (iv) non-governmental organisations

    (v) co-operatives.

(b) Describe the different ways in which organisations may be structured: entrepreneurial, functional, matrix, divisional, departmental, by geographical area and by product. [1]

(c) Describe the roles and functions of the main departments in a business organisation: [1]

    (i) research and development

    (ii) purchasing

    (iii) production

    (iv) direct service provision

    (v) marketing

    (vi) administration

    (vii) finance.

(d) Explain the characteristics of the strategic, tactical and operational levels in the organisation in the context of the Anthony hierarchy. [1]

(e) Explain the role of marketing in an organisation: [1]

    (i) the definition of marketing

    (ii) the marketing mix

    (iii) the relationship of the marketing plan to the strategic plan

(f) Explain basic organisational structure concepts: [2]

    (i) separation of direction and management

    (ii) span of control and scalar chain

    (iii) tall and flat organisations.

(g) Explain centralisation and decentralisation and list their advantages and disadvantages. [1]

2 The formal and informal business organisation

(a) Explain the informal organisation and its relationship with the formal organisation. [1]

(b) Describe the impact of the informal organisation on the business. [2]

3 Organisational culture in business

(a) Define organisational culture. [1]

(b) Describe the factors that shape the culture of the organisation. [1]

(c) Explain the contribution made by writers on culture: [1]

    (i) Schein – determinants of organisational culture

    (ii) Handy – four cultural stereotypes

    (iii) Hofstede – international perspectives on culture.

4 Stakeholders of business organisations

(a) Define the internal stakeholder and list the different categories of internal stakeholder. [1]

(b) Define connected and external stakeholders and explain their impact on the organisation. [1]

(c) Identify the main stakeholder groups and the objectives of each group. [1]

(d) Explain how the different stakeholder groups interact and how their objectives may conflict with one another. [1]

5 Information technology and information systems in business

(a) Discuss the types of information technology and information systems used by the business organisation.[1]

(b) List the attributes of good quality information.[1]

(c) Explain how the type of information differs and the purposes for which it is applied at different levels of the organisation: strategic, tactical and operational.[1]

(d) Identify the different sources of internal and external information.[1]

(e) Describe the main features of information systems used within the organisation.[1]

6 Committees in the business organisation

(a) Explain the purposes of committees.[1]

(b) Describe the types of committee used by business organisations.[1]

(c) List the advantages and disadvantages of committees.[1]

(d) Explain the roles of the Chair and Secretary of a committee.[1]

7 Business ethics and ethical behaviour

(a) Define business ethics and explain the importance of ethics to the organisation and to the individual.[1]

(b) Identify influences that determine whether behaviour and decisions are ethical or unethical.[1]

(c) Identify the factors that distinguish a profession from other types of occupation.[1]

(d) Explain the role of the accountant in promoting ethical behaviour.[1]

(e) Recognise the purpose of international and organisational codes of ethics and codes of conduct, IFAC, ACCA, etc.[1]

8 Governance and social responsibility in business

(a) Recognise the concept of separation between ownership and control.[1]

(b) Define corporate governance and social responsibility and explain their importance in contemporary organisations.[1]

(c) Explain the responsibility of organisations to maintain appropriate standards of corporate governance and corporate social responsibility.[1]

(d) Briefly explain the main recommendations of best practice in effective corporate governance:[1]

(i) non-executive directors

(ii) remuneration committees

(iii) audit committees

(iv) public oversight

(e) Explain how organisations take account of their social responsibility objectives through analysis of the needs of internal, connected and external stakeholders.[1]

(f) Identify the social and environmental responsibilities of business organisations to internal, connected and external stakeholders. [1]

B KEY ENVIRONMENTAL INFLUENCES AND CONSTRAINTS ON BUSINESS AND ACCOUNTING

1 Political and legal factors

(a) Define environmental forces in terms of political, legal, economic, social and technological factors.[1]

(b) Explain how the political system and government policy affect the organisation.[1]

(c) Describe the sources of legal authority, including supra-national bodies, national and regional governments.[1]

(d) Explain how the law protects the employee and the implications of employment legislation for the manager and the organisation.[1]

(e) Identify the principles of data protection and security.[1]

(f) Explain how the law promotes and protects health and safety in the workplace.[1]

(g) Recognise the responsibility of the individual and organisation for compliance with laws on data protection, security and health and safety.[1]

2 Macro-economic factors

(a) Define macro-economic policy.[1]

(b) Explain the main determinants of the level of business activity in the economy and how variations in the level of business activity affect individuals, households and businesses.[1]

(c) Explain the impact of economic issues on the individual, the household and the business: [1]

   (i) inflation

   (ii) unemployment

   (iii) stagnation

   (iv) international payments disequilibrium.

(d) Describe the main types of economic policy that may be implemented by government and supra-national bodies to maximise economic welfare.[1]

(e) Recognise the impact of fiscal and monetary policy measures on the individual, the household and businesses.[1]

3 Social and demographic factors

(a) Explain the medium and long-term effects of social and demographic trends on business outcomes and the economy.[1]

(b) Describe the impact of changes in social structure, values, attitudes and tastes on the organisation.[2]

(c) Identify and explain the measures that governments may take in response to the medium and long-term impact of demographic change.[2]

4 Technological factors

(a) Explain the effects of technological change on the organisation structure and strategy:[1]

   (i) Downsizing

   (ii) Delayering

   (iii) Outsourcing

(b) Describe the impact of information technology and information systems development on business processes.[1]

5 Competitive factors

(a) Explain the factors that influence the level of competitiveness in an industry or sector.[1]

(b) Describe the activities of an organisation that affect its competitiveness:[1]

   (i) purchasing

   (ii) production

   (iii) marketing

   (iv) service

C HISTORY AND ROLE OF ACCOUNTING IN BUSINESS

1 The history and function of accounting in business

(a) Briefly explain the history and development of the accounting and finance role in business.[1]

(b) Explain the overall role and separate functions of the accounting department.[1]

2 Law and regulation governing accounting

(a) Explain basic legal requirements in relation to keeping and submitting proper records and preparing financial accounts.[1]

(b) Explain the broad consequences of failing to comply with the legal requirements for maintaining accounting records.[1]

(c) Explain how the international accountancy profession regulates itself through the establishment of reporting standards and their monitoring.[1]

3 Financial systems, procedures and IT applications

(a) Explain how business and financial systems and procedures are formulated and implemented to reflect the objectives and policies of the organisation.[1]

(b) Describe the main financial systems used within an organisation:[1]

   (i) purchases and sales invoicing

   (ii) payroll

   (iii) credit control

   (iv) cash and working capital management.

(c) Explain why appropriate controls are necessary in relation to business and IT systems and procedures.[2]

(d) Understand business uses of computers and IT software applications:[1]

   (i) Spreadsheet applications

   (ii) Database systems

(e) Describe and compare the relative benefits and limitations of manual and automated financial systems that may be used in an organisation.[2]

4 The relationship between accounting and other business functions

(a) Explain the relationship between accounting and purchasing/procurement.[1]

(b) Explain financial considerations in production and production planning.[1]

(c) Identify the financial issues associated with marketing.[1]

(d) Identify the financial costs and benefits of effective service provision.[1]

D SPECIFIC FUNCTIONS OF ACCOUNTING AND INTERNAL FINANCIAL CONTROL

1 Accounting and finance functions within business

(a) Explain the contribution of the accounting function to the formulation, implementation, and control of the organisation's policies, procedures, and performance.[2]

(b) Identify and describe the main accounting and reporting functions in business:[1]

   (i) recording financial information

   (ii) codifying and processing financial information

   (iii) preparing financial statements

(c) Identify and describe the main management accounting and performance management functions in business:[1]

   (i) recording and analysing costs and revenues

   (ii) providing management accounting information for decision-making

   (iii) planning and preparing budgets and exercising budgetary control.

(d) Identify and describe the main finance and treasury functions:[1]

   (i) calculating and mitigating business tax liabilities

   (ii) evaluating and obtaining finance

   (iii) managing working capital

   (iv) treasury and risk management.

2 Internal and external auditing and their functions

(a) Define internal and external audit.[1]

(b) Explain the main functions of the internal auditor and the external auditor.[1]

3 Internal financial control and security within business organisations

(a) Explain internal control and internal check.[1]

(b) Explain the importance of internal financial controls in an organisation.[2]

(c) Describe the responsibilities of management for internal financial control.[1]

(d) Describe the features of effective internal financial control procedures in an organisation.[2]

(e) Identify and describe features for protecting the security of IT systems and software within business.[1]

(f) Describe general and application systems controls in business.[1]

4 Fraud and fraudulent behaviour and their prevention in business.

(a) Explain the circumstances under which fraud is likely to arise.[1]

(b) Identify different types of fraud in the organisation.[1]

(c) Explain the implications of fraud for the organisation.[2]

(d) Explain the role and duties of individual managers in the fraud detection and prevention process.[1]

E LEADING AND MANAGING INDIVIDUALS AND TEAMS

1 Leadership, management and supervision

(a) Define leadership, management and supervision and the distinction between these terms.[1]

(b) Explain the nature of management:[1]

    (i)   scientific/classical theories of management – Fayol, Taylor

    (ii)   the human relations school – Mayo

    (iii)   the functions of a manager – Mintzberg, Drucker

(c) Explain the areas of managerial authority and responsibility.[2]

(d) Explain the qualities, situational, functional and contingency approaches to leadership with reference to the theories of Adair, Fiedler, Bennis, Kotter and Heifetz.[2]

(e) Explain leadership styles and contexts using the models of Ashridge, and Blake and Mouton.[2]

2 Individual and group behaviour in business organisations

(a) Describe the main characteristics of individual and group behaviour.[1]

(b) Outline the contributions of individuals and teams to organisational success.[1]

(c) Identify individual and team approaches to work.[1]

3 Team formation, development and management

(a) Explain the differences between a group and a team.[1]

(b) Define the purposes of a team.[1]

(c) Explain the role of the manager in building the team and developing individuals within the team.[1]

    (i)   Belbin's team roles theory

    (ii)   Tuckman's theory of team development

(d) List the characteristics of effective and ineffective teams.[1]

(e) Describe tools and techniques that can be used to build the team and improve team effectiveness.[1]

4 Motivating individuals and groups

(a) Define motivation and explain its importance to the organisation, teams and individuals.[1]

(b) Explain content and process theories of motivation – Maslow, Herzberg, McGregor, and Vroom.[2]

(c) Explain and identify types of intrinsic and extrinsic reward.[1]

(d) Explain how reward systems can be designed and implemented to motivate teams and individuals.[1]

F RECRUITING AND DEVELOPING EFFECTIVE EMPLOYEES

1 Recruitment and selection, managing diversity and equal opportunity

(a) Explain the importance of effective recruitment and selection to the organisation.[1]

(b) Describe the recruitment and selection processes and explain the stages in these processes.[1]

(c) Describe the roles of those involved in the recruitment and selection processes.[1]

(d) Describe the methods through which organisations seek to meet their recruitment needs.[1]

(e) Explain the advantages and disadvantages of different recruitment and selection methods.[1]

(f) Explain the purposes of a diversity policy within the human resources plan.[2]

(g) Explain the purpose and benefits of an equal opportunities policy within human resource planning.[2]

(h) Explain the practical steps that an organisation may take to ensure the effectiveness of its diversity and equal opportunities policy.[1]

2 Techniques for improving personal effectiveness at work and their benefits

(a) Explain the purposes of personal development plans.[1]

(b) Describe how a personal development plan should be formulated, implemented, monitored and reviewed by the individual.[1]

(c) Explain the importance of effective time management.[1]

(d) Describe the barriers to effective time management and how they may be overcome.[1]

(e) Describe the role of information technology in improving personal effectiveness.[1]

(f) Explain the purposes and processes of coaching, mentoring and counselling and their benefits.[1]

3 Features of effective communication

(a) Define communications.[1]

(b) Explain a simple communication model: sender, message, receiver, feedback, noise.[1]

(c) Explain formal and informal communication and their importance in the workplace.[1]

(d) Identify the consequences of ineffective communication.[1]

(e) Describe the attributes of effective communication.[1]

(f) Describe the barriers to effective communication and identify practical steps that may be taken to overcome them.[1]

(g) Describe the main methods and patterns of communication.[1]

4 Training, development and learning in the maintenance and improvement of business performance

(a) Explain the importance of learning in the workplace.[2]

(b) Describe the learning process – Honey and Mumford, Kolb.[1]

(c) Describe the role of the human resources department and individual managers in the learning process.[1]

(d) Describe the training and development process: identifying needs, setting objectives, programme design, delivery and validation.[1]

(e) Explain the terms 'training', 'development' and 'education', and the characteristics of each.[1]

(f) List the benefits of effective training and development in the workplace.[1]

5 Review and appraisal of individual performance

(a) Explain the importance of performance assessment.[1]

(b) Explain how organisations assess the performance of human resources.[1]

(c) Define performance appraisal and describe its purposes.[1]

(d) Describe the performance appraisal process.[1]

(e) Explain the benefits of effective appraisal.[2]

(f) Identify the barriers to effective appraisal and how these may be overcome.[1]

(g) Explain how the effectiveness of performance appraisal may be evaluated.[2]

ANALYSIS OF PILOT PAPERS

June 2007

The examiner has suggested that the pilot paper is a good representation of the forthcoming examinations. It covered all syllabus areas and consisted of 40 two mark questions and 10 one mark questions.

KAPLAN PUBLISHING

REVISION GUIDANCE

Planning your revision

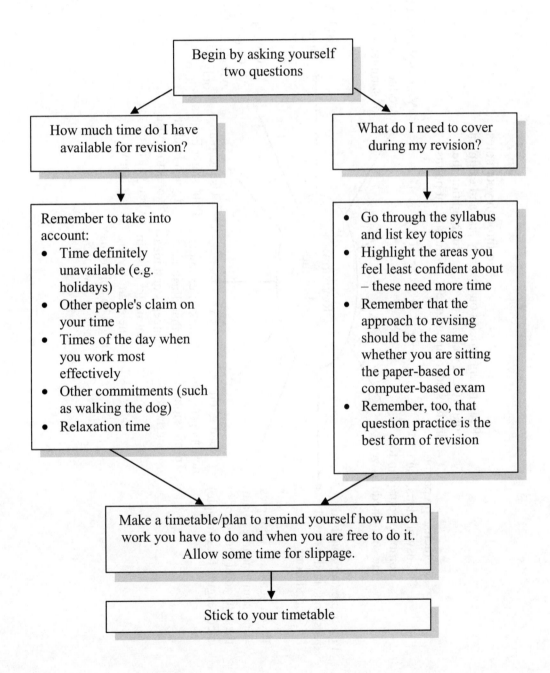

Begin by asking yourself two questions

How much time do I have available for revision?

What do I need to cover during my revision?

Remember to take into account:
- Time definitely unavailable (e.g. holidays)
- Other people's claim on your time
- Times of the day when you work most effectively
- Other commitments (such as walking the dog)
- Relaxation time

- Go through the syllabus and list key topics
- Highlight the areas you feel least confident about – these need more time
- Remember that the approach to revising should be the same whether you are sitting the paper-based or computer-based exam
- Remember, too, that question practice is the best form of revision

Make a timetable/plan to remind yourself how much work you have to do and when you are free to do it. Allow some time for slippage.

Stick to your timetable

Revision techniques

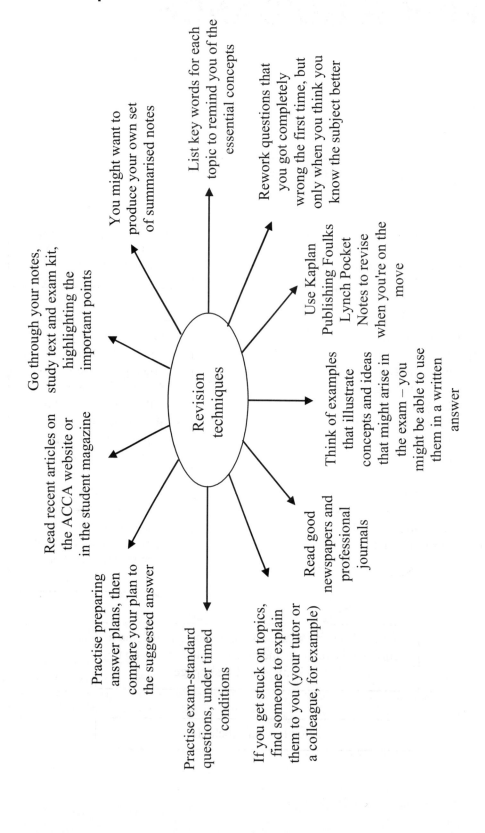

Revision techniques

List key words for each topic to remind you of the essential concepts

Rework questions that you got completely wrong the first time, but only when you think you know the subject better

You might want to produce your own set of summarised notes

Go through your notes, study text and exam kit, highlighting the important points

Use Kaplan Publishing Foulks Lynch Pocket Notes to revise when you're on the move

Read recent articles on the ACCA website or in the student magazine

Think of examples that illustrate concepts and ideas that might arise in the exam – you might be able to use them in a written answer

Practise preparing answer plans, then compare your plan to the suggested answer

Read good newspapers and professional journals

Practise exam-standard questions, under timed conditions

If you get stuck on topics, find someone to explain them to you (your tutor or a colleague, for example)

EXAM TECHNIQUES

Paper-based exams – tips

- You might want to spend the first few minutes of the exam **reading the paper**.

- Where you have a **choice of question**, decide which questions you will do.

- Unless you know exactly how to answer the question, spend some time **planning** your answer.

- **Divide the time** you spend on questions in proportion to the marks on offer. One suggestion is to allocate 1½ minutes to each mark available, so a 10 mark question should be completed in 15 minutes.

- Spend the last **five minutes** reading through your answers and **making any additions or corrections**.

- If you **get completely stuck** with a question, leave space in your answer book and **return to it later.**

- Stick to the question and **tailor your answer** to what you are asked. Pay particular attention to the verbs in the question.

- If you do not understand what a question is asking, **state your assumptions**. Even if you do not answer in precisely the way the examiner hoped, you should be given some credit, if your assumptions are reasonable.

- You should do everything you can to make things easy for the marker. The marker will find it easier to identify the points you have made if your **answers are legible**.

- **Essay questions**: Your essay should have a clear structure. It should contain a brief introduction, a main section and a conclusion. Be concise. It is better to write a little about a lot of different points than a great deal about one or two points.

- **Multiple-choice questions**: don't treat these as an easy option – you could lose marks by rushing into your answer. Read the questions carefully and work through any calculations required. If you don't know the answer, eliminate those options you know are incorrect and see if the answer becomes more obvious.

- **Objective test questions** might ask for numerical answers, but could also involve paragraphs of text which require you to fill in a number of missing blanks, or for you to write a definition of a word or phrase. Others may give a definition followed by a list of possible key words relating to that description. Whatever the format, these questions require that you have *learnt* definitions, *know* key words and their meanings and importance, and *understand* the names and meanings of rules, concepts and theories.

- **Computations**: It is essential to include all your workings in your answers. Many computational questions require the use of a standard format: company profit and loss account, balance sheet and cash flow statement for example. Be sure you know these formats thoroughly before the exam and use the layouts that you see in the answers given in this book and in model answers.

- **Case studies**: to write a good case study, first identify the area in which there is a problem, outline the main principles/theories you are going to use to answer the question, and then apply the principles/theories to the case.

- **Reports, memos and other documents**: some questions ask you to present your answer in the form of a report, memo or other document. So use the correct format – there could be easy marks to gain here.

Computer-based exams – tips

- Be sure you understand how to use the **software** before you start the exam. If in doubt, ask the assessment centre staff to explain it to you.

- Questions are **displayed on the screen** and answers are entered using keyboard and mouse. At the end of the exam, you are given a certificate showing the result you have achieved.

- In addition to the traditional multiple-choice question type, CBEs might also contain **other types of questions**, such as number entry questions, formula entry questions, and stem questions with multiple parts. There are also questions that carry several marks.

- You need to be sure you **know how to answer questions** of this type before you sit the exam, through practice.

- Do not attempt a CBE until you have **completed all study material** relating to it.

- **Do not skip any of the material** in the syllabus.

- **Read each question** *very* carefully.

- **Double-check your answer** before committing yourself to it.

- Answer *every* question – if you do not know an answer, you don't lose anything by guessing. Think carefully before you **guess**.

- If you are answering a multiple-choice question, eliminate first those answers that you know are wrong. Then choose the most appropriate answer from those that are left.

- Remember that **only one answer to a multiple-choice question can be right**. After you have eliminated the ones that you know to be wrong, if you are still unsure, guess. oOly guess after you have double-checked that you have only eliminated answers that are *definitely* wrong.

- **Don't panic** if you realise you've answered a question incorrectly. Getting one question wrong will not mean the difference between passing and failing.

Section 1

PRACTICE QUESTIONS

THE BUSINESS ORGANISATION

1   Considering the variety of organisational objectives, for a company with a strong focus on ethical behaviour, which of the following would be given particular attention during target-setting process?

   A   Efficiency of operations

   B   Innovation and learning

   C   Social responsibility

   D   Employee retention   **(2 marks)**

2   Which of the following organisations is normally found in the public sector?

   A   Education

   B   Charities

   C   Clubs

   D   Businesses   **(2 marks)**

3   The public sector is normally concerned with:

   A   making profit from the sale of goods

   B   providing services to specific groups funded from charitable donations

   C   the provision of basic government services

   D   raising funds by subscriptions from members to provide common services   **(2 marks)**

4   Private limited companies, partnerships, publicly-owned companies and public limited companies would all be considered as private sector organisations.

   Is this statement rue or false?   **(1 mark)**

5   Two people are the only shareholders in a limited liability company. This means that:

   A   they must meet all the debts of the company

   B   the company cannot become bankrupt

   C   they cannot be asked to meet the debts of the company

   D   the business has a turnover of less than £100,000   **(2 marks)**

6   When considering the roles of different departments, which one of the following is likely to be concerned with identifying and satisfying customer needs?

    A   Production

    B   Research and Development

    C   Marketing

    D   Purchasing   **(2 marks)**

7   Which of the following organisations could be said to be owned and democratically controlled by its members?

    A   Schools

    B   Council

    C   A Co-operative

    D   A small private limited company   **(2 marks)**

8   A method of coordination used by many fast-food chains to deliver greater efficiency is

    A   standardisation

    B   co-operation

    C   staff handbooks

    D   yearly meetings   **(2 marks)**

9   Which of the following is one of the three distinct steps in the strategic planning process?

    A   Organic growth v acquisition strategy

    B   Stakeholder analysis

    C   Production of plans for all key functions

    D   Strategic choice   **(2 marks)**

10   Which of the following is one of the three planning levels?

    A   Divisional planning

    B   Functional planning

    C   Operational planning

    D   Resource planning   **(2 marks)**

11   When considering the reasons why organisations are created, which of the following is false?

    A   Organisations allow people to decrease the amount of individual responsibility and therefore limit exposure to risk

    B   By pooling ideas together people are able to achieve more than each of them could have achieved individually

    C   On joining the organisation, people become less powerful as it makes it harder to realise one's ideas   **(1 mark)**

12   Specialisation was first used in car production at Ford and is associated with the work of ....

Which word completes this sentence?

A   Taylor

B   Ford

C   Mintzberg   **(1 mark)**

ORGANISATIONAL STRUCTURE

13   The entrepreneurial structure is typical of which of the following?

A   Large, successful, companies dominated by a powerful individual

B   Small companies in their early days

C   Risk taking companies of all sizes

D   Fast growing companies   **(2 marks)**

14   The staff of Lively shares a lot of common interests and often meets socially both inside and outside work. The grapevine is regarded by many staff as the most reliable source of company information and the staff has developed their own approach to many aspects of their work. This form of organisational arrangement is characteristic of which of the following?

A   Decentralisation

B   Divorce of ownership and control

C   Wide span of control

D   The informal organisation   **(2 marks)**

15   Which of the following is a disadvantage of a functional structure?

A   Lack of economies of scale

B   Absence of standardisation

C   Specialists feel isolated

D   Empire building   **(2 marks)**

16   Which of the following structures is best placed to address the need for co-ordination in very complex situations?

A   Functional

B   Divisional

C   Matrix

D   Geographical   **(2 marks)**

17   The scalar chain shows the number of people for whom a manager is directly responsible.

Is this statement true or false?   **(1 mark)**

18 When considering the need for workforce flexibility, which of the following would be classed as functional flexibility?

A Organisation can easily decrease or increase the number of people on the payroll

B Subcontracting or automating part of the production process

C Training staff so they are multi-skilled

D Ensuring that necessary financial resources can be obtained when needed **(2 marks)**

19 The term 'networking' is most associated with what type of organisational structure?

A Functional

B Entrepreneurial

C Matrix

D Divisional **(2 marks)**

20 Which of the following structures results in a potential loss of control over key operating decisions?

A Matrix

B Entrepreneurial

C Functional

D Geographic **(2 marks)**

21 One of the main reasons for the separation of ownership and management of larger organisations is that the managers do not have access to sufficient funds.

Is this statement true or false? **(1 mark)**

22 What impact will there be on manager's span of control if the people he/she is managing are located in different geographical areas?

A No impact

B It is likely to increase

C It is likely to decrease

D Chain of command will collapse **(2 marks)**

23 Which of the following is an advantage of decentralisation?

A Better local decisions

B Increased goal congruence

C More experienced managers

D Reduced training costs **(2 marks)**

ORGANISATIONAL CULTURE

24 Culture was expressed by Handy as 'the sum total of the belief, knowledge, attitudes, norms and customs that prevail in an organisation'?

Is this statement true or false?   **(1 mark)**

25 The tales of company creation, such as difficulties the founder had to face and how he/she managed to overcome them successfully often form a part of organisational culture.

Is this statement true or false?

(1 mark)

26 Which of the following is one of the three levels of culture described by Schein?

A   Things that are inspirational, such as slogans and mission statements

B   Things that can be easily seen, such as the way people dress

C   Things that endure, such as organisational hierarchy

D   Things that initially appear superficial, such as timekeeping rules   **(2 marks)**

27 Which of the following is one of the four cultural types identified by Handy?

A   Growth culture

B   Purposeful culture

C   Person culture

D   Inclusive culture   **(2 marks)**

28 According to Handy's theory, in the person culture which of the following would be correct?

A   Contribution made by each employee is recognised and appreciated

B   The status symbols are there to remind staff of their place

C   People believe that if they meet their job requirement, they will slowly progress to the senior management

D   Rules are put in place and must be strictly followed by all   **(2 marks)**

29 Hofstede found that some cultures (e.g. France and Japan) use bureaucracy to reduce .... because they dislike it.

Which word correctly completes this sentence?

A   Informality

B   Uncertainty

C   Imprecision   **(1 mark)**

LEADERSHIP, MANAGEMENT AND SUPERVISION

30   Adair's action-centred leadership model can be considered to be part of which of the following schools of thought?

    A   Human relations school

    B   Classical school

    C   Contingency school

    D   Scientific school   **(2 marks)**

31   When a situation is either very favourable or very unfavourable to the leader (e.g. the leader is not liked and the leader's power to reward or punish is limited), Fiedler suggested that which of the following styles works best?

    A   Psychologically close

    B   Psychologically open

    C   Psychologically committed

    D   Psychologically distant   **(2 marks)**

32   Old Metalbashers is unprofitable and its turnover is declining, but the employees are reluctant to adopt new technology and unwilling to attend re- training courses. They see no need to change. According to Heifetz which sort of change is necessary in this situation?

    A   Technical

    B   Adaptive

    C   Fundamental

    D   Psychological   **(2 marks)**

33   Leadership is an .... influence directed toward the achievement of a goal or goals.

    Which word correctly completes this definition of leadership?

    A   Positive

    B   Multifaceted

    C   Interpersonal   **(1 mark)**

34   Management can be defined as 'the effective use of ...., such as capital, plant, materials and labour, to achieve defined objectives with maximum efficiency'.

    Which word correctly completes this definition of management?

    A   Resources

    B   Facilities

    C   Assets   **(1 mark)**

35   **The main role of a supervisor is best described as:**

A   a negotiator of industrial relations within a department

B   someone to resolve problems first hand where the work is done

C   someone to ensure that specified tasks are performed correctly and efficiently

D   the interface between the management and the workforce   **(2 marks)**

36   **Fayol and Taylor shared the belief that:**

A   employees work better if they are given a wide range of tasks to complete

B   management must gain trust and persuade others to follow

C   changing the corporate culture is the most important avenue of change

D   individuals must subordinate themselves to the needs of the organisation   **(2 marks)**

37   **Which of these steps aimed at increasing job satisfaction could be attributed to the findings of the human relation school?**

A   Creating an open-office environment so people can socialise more freely

B   Paying staff for each hour worked or item produced

C   Managers setting challenging individual targets

D   Producing an organisational chart so staff are aware of where they stand in the hierarchy

(2 marks)

38   **Contingency theorists believe that:**

A   effective management is primarily a function of successful people management

B   organisational achievement is largely contingent upon general economic circumstances

C   major change is dependent primarily upon clarity and communication of the strategic vision

D   lessons of earlier theorists should be adapted to suit particular circumstances

(2 marks)

39   **Which of the following contains the three categories used by Mintzberg to group the ten skills managers need?**

A   Tactical; Operational; Strategic

B   Communication; Control; Vision

C   Interpersonal; Informational; Decisional

D   Objectives; Direction; Drive   **(2 marks)**

40   **Fayol defined authority as the right to give orders and the power to exact obedience.**

Is this statement true or false?   **(1 mark)**

41 Which of the following are the three types of authority a manager or department may often be said to have?

A   Legitimate, Referent, Expert

B   Direct, Indirect, Delegated

C   Assumed, Imposed, natural

D   Line, Staff, Functional   **(2 marks)**

42 A manager possessing which of the following types of power will be able to exercise a strong influence on his staff so they will identify with him and try to act in the way he would wish them to.

A   Legitimate

B   Resource

C   Referent

D   Reward   **(2 marks)**

43 Every person in an organisation, including the Senior Management Team and the Board of Directors, has both responsibility and accountability.

Is this statement true or false?   **(1 mark)**

44 The trait theories of leadership were based around which of the following groups of qualities?

A   Intelligence; Rationality; Decisiveness

B   Physical; Personality; Social

C   Empathy; Inspiration; Courage

D   Aggression; Negotiation; Vision   **(2 marks)**

45 In the context of Blake and Mouton's grid a manager in the top left hand corner of the grid (Square 1.9) would fall into which of the following categories?

A   Management impoverished

B   'Country Club'

C   Task management

D   Team management   **(2 marks)**

46 Which of the following sets out the four management styles identified by Ashridge Management College?

A   Objective, Negotiator, Diplomatic, Decisive

B   Aggressive, Reasonable, Visionary, Pragmatic

C   Tells, Sells, Consults, Joins

D   Thinks, Considers, Negotiates, Resolves   **(2 marks)**

INDIVIDUAL AND GROUP BEHAVIOUR IN BUSINESS ORGANISATIONS

47   When checking sales records of the company, a junior member of staff has uncovered a suspicious irregularity in the way transactions are processed. This would need more time to be investigated fully, however the audit manager is stressing the need to meet the tight deadline for completion. Using the role theory, this could be referred to as:

    A   role ambiguity

    B   sole sign

    C   role behaviour

    D   role conflict   **(2 marks)**

48   What are the three different types of behaviour that can be adopted when dealing with other people?

    A   Enquiring; Negotiating; Resolving

    B   Thoughtful; Emotional; Responsive

    C   Considerate; Positive; Directed

    D   Assertive; Aggressive; Passive   **(2 marks)**

49   Synergy describes the phenomenon where:

    A   collaboration leads to high levels of output

    B   more energy is output than is input

    C   sun spots drive turbulent business conditions on earth

    D $2 + 2 = 5$ **(2 marks)**

50   The factors required to make a cohesive group are best represented in which of the following?

    A   Right mix of skills/Leadership/Clear objectives

    B   Negotiation/Dealing with challenging tasks/Shared objectives

    C   Shared values/Preference for formal meetings only/Openness

    D   Determination/Empathy/Emphasis on following rules   **(2 marks)**

TEAM FORMATION, DEVELOPMENT AND MANAGEMENT

51   A group is best described as any collection of people that:

    A   has been formed with a particular objective in mind

    B   has a distinctive culture

    C   is focused on an end result

    D   sees themselves as a group   **(2 marks)**

52 **A team is a formal group**

Is this statement true or false? **(2 marks)**

53 **The basic purpose of a team is best described as:**

A working together to resolve problems quickly and efficiently

B achieving a shared goal by shared means and enthusiasms

C solving complex problems through synergy and a team of specialists

D identifying, investigating and removing the underlying cause of a problem **(2 marks)**

54 **Which of the following includes three of the roles Belbin suggested a group needs in order to be effective?**

A Leader, Shaper, Plant

B Negotiator; Finisher; Initiator

C Co-ordinator; Progress chaser; Diplomat

D Finisher; Block remover; Negotiator **(2 marks)**

55 **Match the following team roles with the appropriate personality.**

(i) Sahra is a very quite person, she often reserves her opinion until being directly asked for it, however she always offers unusual and creative suggestions when the team is faced with difficult problem

(ii) Jim is respected by all team members for his analytical skills, though he rarely gets invited to out-of-office private parties as many find him tactless

(iii) Esther is the company's HR manager, she ensures that any potential conflicts are promptly identified and resolved and the team members work harmoniously

Options:

A 1 – Shaper, 2 – Leader, 3 – Company worker

B 1 – Plant, 2 – Finisher, 3 – Team worker

C 1 – Plant, 2 – Monitor-Evaluator, 3 – Team worker

D 1 – Resource-Investigator, 2 – Shaper, 3 – Company worker **(2 marks)**

56 **At which stage of team development, according to Tuckman, will the effectiveness of work be at the lowest point?**

A Forming

B Storming

C Norming

D Performing **(2 marks)**

57   The fifth stage which has been added to Tuckman's four stages of team development is:

A   Warming

B   Reforming

C   Dorming

D   Leading   **(2 marks)**

MOTIVATING INDIVIDUALS AND GROUPS

58   Which of the following types of incentives aimed at improving performance will be most appropriate in a professional office environment, for example in the HR department staff?

A   Commission

B   Piece rate

C   Profit sharing

D   Productivity plans   **(2 marks)**

59   Profit sharing is not a good way of rewarding the particular achievements of individual employees.

Is this statement true or false?   **(1 mark)**

60   Motivation refers to how hard you are willing to work whilst satisfaction refers to your contentment with your job.

Is this statement true or false?   **(2 marks)**

61   Content theories focus manager's attention of the calculation process that takes place when people decide whether certain rewards are worthwhile. Process theories assume all people are the same; therefore a standard set of incentives could be applied to meet staff needs.

Is this statement true or false   **(1 mark)**

62   Which of the following would fit into Maslow's Ego category?

A   Loss of one's home

B   Winning a prize

C   A salary increase

D   An invitation to a party   **(2 marks)**

63   Maslow's theory can be summarised by saying that the things people need can be placed in .... ascending categories.

Which word completes this statement?

A   Three

B   Four

C   Five   **(1 mark)**

64 According to Herzberg, which of the following job design methods can yield a significant long-term improvement in employee satisfaction?

    A   Job enlargement

    B   Job rotation

    C   Job enrichment

    D   Job switching   **(2 marks)**

65 If you believe that you have Theory Y workers, you would adopt an authoritarian, repressive style with tight control.

Is this statement true or false?   **(1 mark)**

66 According to Douglas McGregor, Theory X people are motivated by:

    A   money and security

    B   achievement at work

    C   interpersonal relationships

    D   recognition for good work   **(2 marks)**

67 'People are motivated by the pursuit of gain and self-interest, so rewards should be based on recognising individual performance'. This management idea best describes:

    A   Maslow's primary needs

    B   Herzberg hygiene factors

    C   McGregor Theory X

    D   Herzberg theory of job design   **(2 marks)**

68 Vroom believes that people will be motivated to do things to reach a goal if they believe in the worth of that goal and:

    A   its achievement will not involve excessive risk

    B   its achievement will not be accompanied by any significant costs

    C   can see that what they do has no substantial downside

    D   can see that what they do will help them in achieving it   **(2 marks)**

69 Extrinsic rewards are those that arise from the performance of the work itself.

Is this statement true or false?   **(1 mark)**

70 Which one of the following is a problem associated with the usage of Management by Objectives approach?

    A   There is very frequent contact and communication between management and staff

    B   The assessment results are agreed by both manager and subordinates

    C   There is a lot of pressure to achieve targets

    D   Employees are involved in decision making   **(2 marks)**

INFORMATION TECHNOLOGY AND INFORMATION SYSTEMS IN BUSINESS

71 An intranet site could be accessed by certain authorised third parties, such as suppliers, to check what policies an organisation has with regards to ordering its materials.

Is this statement true or false? **(1 mark)**

72 Information is data that has been processed in such a way that it has a .... to the person who receives it, who may then use it to improve the quality of decision making

Which word correctly completes this definition?

A Meaning

B Usefulness

C Significance **(1 mark)**

73 Which of the following statements shows how computerisation has influenced the quality of information provision within an organisation?

A An accountant has thechance to quickly reverse the entries before a supervisor can notice

B It did not result in any improvements as the month end still takes ages to prepare for

C The volume of transactions staff has to cope with became overwhelming

D The speed of processing has increased with the information being instantly available at one's finger tips **(2 mark)**

74 Which of the following contains four of the eight qualities of good information?

A Useful, Helpful, Accurate, Low cost

B Versatile, Reliable, Relevant, Timely

C Accurate, Complete, Understandable, Relevant

D Brief, Complete, Specific, Timeless **(2 marks)**

75 Decision making and the information required to support it have been analysed into three levels; which of the following contains these three levels?

A Strategic, Functional, Detail

B Board, Management, Operations

C Complex, Straightforward, Detail

D Strategic, Tactical, Operational **(2 marks)**

76 Which of the following four system types found within most management information systems would provide reports on activities such as output levels, sales ledger and credit accounts in arrears?

A   Database systems

B   Direct control systems

C   Enquiry systems

D   Support systems   **(2 marks)**

77 Which of the following sources of information would be considered internal?

A   Interviewing potential customers

B   Reading business magazines

C   Receiving updates from tax authorities

D   Looking through sales records for the last year   **(2 marks)**

78 Purchase ledger, sales ledger and payroll systems are examples of which kind of information system?

A   Executive information systems

B   Decision support systems

C   Transaction processing systems

D   Management information systems   **(2 marks)**

79 Which of the following converts data from a transaction processing system into information for monitoring performance, maintaining co-ordination and providing background information?

A   Expert systems

B   Decision support systems

C   Executive information systems

D   Management information systems   **(2 marks)**

80 When the government authority at the end of a tax year sends thousands of notifications to people with the estimate of the tax they need to pay, these letters are likely to be produced by:

A   Decision Support System

B   Executive Information system

C   Expert system

D   Management Information System   **(2 marks)**

81 Which of the following is a reasonable drawback of using a database?

A   System failures are likely to be widespread

B   It is difficult for two people to use it at the same time

C   The quantity of information is limited to just a few thousand records

D   Costs of setting it up are likely to outweigh the benefits of using it   **(2 marks)**

82   Which information system monitors both the internal and external environment of the company and gives access to information at the tactical and strategic levels?

      A   Decision support systems

      B   Executive information systems

      C   Expert systems

      D   Management information systems   **(2 marks)**

POLITICAL AND LEGAL FACTORS

83   Which of the following would a haulage company monitor under the Political heading as part of a PEST analysis?

      A   Tracking systems to monitor driver hours/anti-theft devices/developments in tyre technology

      B   State of the economy/oil price movements/a rise in interest rates

      C   Fuel tax/congestion charges in cities/plans to build new roads

      D   Predicted car numbers and usage/public concerns over safety   **(2 marks)**

84   A political system can be defined as 'A complete set of institutions, political organisations, interest groups, the relationships between those institutions and the political norms and rules that govern their functions'.

      Is this statement true or false?   **(1 mark)**

85   Which of the following actions is often associated with lobby groups?

      A   Attempting to influence a governmental official and persuade her to take issues such as global warming seriously

      B   Building an extensive entranceway to a house as to accommodate a whole group of people

      C   Pursuing a leisurely activity, such as golf

      D   issuing a notice of prohibition of trade by a court   **(2 marks)**

86   Nationalisation of an industry often involves government selling some of its assets in a bid to promote competition.

      Is this statement true or false?   **(1 mark)**

87   Which firms are affected by legislation protecting employee rights, consumers and the environment?

      A   Limited companies only

      B   Firms of a certain size

      C   Firms in certain industries

      D   All firms   **(2 marks)**

88   Supra-national sources of legal authority include:

A   A United Nations resolution

B   US legislation

C   UK Government legislation

D   High court in London   **(2 marks)**

89   The Data Protection act focuses on:

A   issues concerning data held about incorporated entities

B   rights of the individual with regards to withholding information about oneself

C   the way data about the individual is to be obtained, used and stored

D   aligning the information requirements between different countries   **(2 marks)**

90   Which of the following contains four of the seven rights of individuals with respect to information stored about them?

A   Right to: seek compensation; take action to rectify, block erase or destroy personal data; prevent processing for direct marketing; prevent decisions against an individual by purely automated means

B   Right to: obtain access to data held overseas; take action to destroy personal data; prevent processing for direct marketing; inspect data in situ in the UK

C   Right to: seek compensation; travel abroad to inspect personal data; inspect personal data in situ in the UK; take action to destroy personal data

D   Right to: destroy hard disks holding personal data; inspect personal data where it is held in the UK; seek compensation; prevent processing for direct marketing.

                                                                                (2 marks)

91   In a typical office environment, it is highly unlikely that any of the Health and Safety Act provisions would be relevant.

        Is this statement true or false?   **(1 mark)**

92   The employee is not responsible for his/her safety at work.

        Is this statement true or false?   **(1 mark)**

MACROECONOMIC FACTORS

93   Which of the following is the name given to unemployment which is the result of aggregate demand in the economy being too small to create employment opportunities for all those willing, and able, to work?

A   Structural unemployment

B   Cyclical unemployment

C   Frictional unemployment

D   Transitional unemployment   **(2 marks)**

94 Countries which enjoy a very large trade surplus (e.g. China) sometimes come under pressure from their trading partners to reduce this surplus by:

A   increasing their exchange rate

B   expenditure reducing strategies

C   expenditure switching strategies

D   lowering their exchange rate   **(2 marks)**

95 Microeconomics is the study of the economic behaviour of:

A   governments

B   small firms

C   individual firms

D   microbes   **(2 marks)**

96 Which of the following lists four typical macroeconomic policy objectives of governments?

A   Profits, Taxation, Employment, Trade surplus

B   Interest rates, Employment, Balance of payments, Growth

C   Revenue, Confidence, Budget surplus, Money supply

D   Growth, Inflation, Unemployment, Balance of payments   **(2 marks)**

97 Which of the following would best summarise the effect of expectations on country's economy?

A   Expectations effect has no influence of the economic development

B   If a government is expecting the citizens' incomes to rise, it will try to adjust the taxation levels as to decrease the amount to be collected

C   If a company expects its trade contract to be terminated, it will take actions to find another customer

D   If people collectively expect the economy to develop in a certain way, they will act in a manner that will facilitate this change   **(2 marks)**

98 What fiscal policy would be best used when trying to address a deflationary gap?

A   Running a budget surplus

B   Having a budget deficit

C   Lowering interest rates

D   Raising interest rates   **(2 marks)**

99 When the economy is in depression, such as for example in USA in 1930s , Keynes suggested that using supply side policies would enable it to recover.

Is this statement true or false?   **(1 mark)**

100 Increases in unemployment, reduced demand, falling household incomes and low business confidence and investment are associated most strongly with which of the following?

    A   High interest rates

    B   Increase in the money supply

    C   A budget deficit

    D   Recession   **(2 marks)**

101 Inflation hits which group the hardest?

    A   The poor and those on fixed incomes

    B   Individuals with substantial share portfolios

    C   Small businesses

    D   Large businesses   **(2 marks)**

102 In the UK who is responsible for setting interest rates?

    A   The Chancellor of the Exchequer

    B   The Bank of England

    C   The Prime Minister

    D   The European Central Bank   **(2 marks)**

103 The balance of payment surplus will result in:

    A   lower rate of economic growth

    B   inflation

    C   unemployment

    D   budget deficit   **(2 marks)**

104 A regressive tax is one which:

    A   takes the same proportion of income as tax across all income levels

    B   takes a higher proportion of a poor person's salary than a rich person's

    C   takes a higher proportion of a rich person's salary than a poor person's.

    D   takes a higher proportion of income in tax as incomes increase   **(2 marks)**

105 Economic growth is measured by:

    A   increases in the average wage level

    B   increases in the physical and financial assets owned by the population

    C   increases in the real (inflation adjusted) gross national product per head of the population

    D   increases in the average profits achieved by firms.   **(2 marks)**

106 The disadvantages of growth include which one of the following:

A   growth rates may exceed inflation rates

B   the gap between rich and poor may narrow

C   growth may exceed population growth

D   growth may be in 'demerit' goods   **(2 marks)**

107 Demand side policies are best described as:

A   a belief that government should manipulate its spending so as to manage aggregate demand

B   ensuring that demand is contained so that inflation is controlled

C   managing down excessive growth by reducing government borrowing

D   keeping employment levels substantially below full levels   **(2 marks)**

108 Monetarist solutions to economic problems are often described as supply side economics?

Is this statement true or false?   **(1 mark)**

109 Which of the following best defines the factors of production?

A   Salaries, Rents, Dividends, Profits

B   Wages, Dividends, Profits, Rents

C   Companies, Buildings, Interest, Wages

D   Labour, Land, Capital, Entrepreneurship   **(2 marks)**

110 Which of the following includes all five causes of inflation?

A   Exported/Cost pull/Demand push/Monetary/Anticipations

B   Expectations/Cost push/Imported/Monetary/Demand pull

C   Greed/Cost pull/Demand pull/Monetary/Imported

D   Money supply/Fears/Demand/Costs/Employment   **(2 marks)**

SOCIAL AND TECHNOLOGICAL FACTORS

111 Nowadays, in developed countries, governmental policy with relations to demographics is more likely to be:

A   encouraging early retirement so young people can find jobs easier

B   promoting consumerism and accumulation of debt

C   making it easier for women to come back to work after having children

D   introducing regulations to restrict the number of local nationals a company can employ   **(2 marks)**

112 Outsourcing is often associated with which business processes?

    A   Allowing employees to work from home

    B   Sourcing data from outside the company

    C   Transferring call centres oversees

    D   Sending staff on foreign assignments   **(2 marks)**

113 Many countries are finding the demand for housing growing faster than the population

Is this statement true or false?   **(1 mark)**

114 The average age of a mother on the birth of their first child has risen in many countries. This has affected demand for better-quality clothing, prams, etc in which of the following ways?

    A   Demand has fallen

    B   Demand has increased

    C   Demand has not changed

    D   Demand has fallen sharply   **(2 marks)**

115 What change in people's attitudes has put additional pressure on businesses to become more socially responsible?

    A   The disposable income is growing as people have fewer children

    B   Urbanisation encourages companies to build more compact offices

    C   Fashion changes rapidly therefore frequently change of suppliers becomes a necessity

    D   People are more aware of the 'carbon footprint' left by a company's operations   **(2 marks)**

116 Introduction of a new technology means that a company can streamline its operations. This impacts organisational structure by:

    A   encouraging managers to spend more time controlling staff activities

    B   allowing the company to reorganise itself into a taller structure

    C   delayering by widening a manager's span of control

    D   proving an opportunity for a company trading on the internet as well as on the High Street   **(2 marks)**

COMPETITIVE FACTORS

117 In Porter's five forces model, the fact that other products offer high quality at a comparable price, would be included under the heading of:

    A   barriers to entry

    B   power of suppliers

    C   threat of substitutes

    D   power of buyers   **(2 marks)**

118 **When assessing an organisation's ability to compete, the main issues to consider are whether:**

    A   the industry is growing or in decline

    B   the profitability of the industry is sufficient to sustain new entrants

    C   new entrants outnumber those leaving the industry

    D   the firm has a sustainable competitive advantage   **(2 marks)**

119 **According to Michael Porter, a firm wishing to obtain a competitive advantage over its rivals is facedwith which of the following two choices?**

    A   Price leadership v Low cost and Degree of differentiation

    B   Cost leadership v Differentiation and Degree of focus

    C   Cost focus v Differentiation focus and Cost leadership v Volume

    D   Differentiation v Volume and Degree of focus   **(2 marks)**

120 **The focus competitive strategy means that a company is targeting a single segment of the market and is able to tailor-make its offerings to the needs of the chosen customer group.**

Is this statement true or false?   **(1 mark)**

121 **When considering Porter's value chain analysis, outbound logistics is:**

    A   receiving, handling and distributing inputs to the production system

    B   using rational approach to solving problems

    C   informing customers about the products a company has to offer

    D   distributing the products to the customer   **(2 marks)**

122 **Porter's five forces collectively determine which of the following:**

    A   the degree of competition new entrants will face

    B   the profitability of existing firms in the industry

    C   the overall growth of the industry

    D   the overall profit potential of the industry   **(2 marks)**

123 **Porter's value chain determines whether and how a firm's activities contribute to which of the following?**

    A   its long term survival

    B   its competitive advantage

    C   its profitability

    D   its productive capacity   **(2 marks)**

STAKEHOLDERS

124   Employees and finance providers belong to which two of the following stakeholder groups?

    A   Internal, Connected

    B   External, Internal

    C   Connected, Outsiders

    D   Internal, Suppliers   **(2 marks)**

125   When analysing stakeholder needs, the group of stakeholders that is likely to be most financially dependent on company's ability to make a profit would include:

    A   pressure groups

    B   customers

    C   employees

    D   tax authorities   **(2 marks)**

126   The interests of customers and shareholders can often appear to conflict.

Is this statement true or false?   **(1 mark)**

127   A is a large company whose shares are owned by a large number of individual investors, who do not wish to engage with company's decision making despite having full rights to do so. When using Mendelow's matrix this stakeholder group would be classed as:

    A   minimal effort

    B   keep informed

    C   keep satisfied

    D   key players   **(2 marks)**

128   When a company uses a communication strategy aimed at explaining the rational behind its actions to its stakeholders, this is referred to by Mendelow as minimal effort approach.

Is this statement true or false?   **(1 mark)**

COMMITTEES IN THE BUSINESS ORGANISATION

129   Which of the following types of committee is often temporary in nature:

    A   ad-hoc committee

    B   standing committee

    C   executive committee

    D   work safety committee   **(2 marks)**

130 **Which of the following would normally be included in the role of a Committee Chairman?**

    A   Making administrative arrangements

    B   Dealing with correspondence

    C   Issuing agenda

    D   Ensuring correct procedures are followed   **(2 marks)**

131 **The duties of the committee secretary include which of the following?**

    A   Making notes/Issuing documents/Fixing date, time, location/Deciding who is to speak

    B   Fixing date, time, location/Making notes/Issuing documents/Preparing minutes

    C   Making notes/Issuing documents/Preparing minutes/Maintaining order

    D   Issuing documents/Fixing date, time, location/Ascertaining the consensus view/Preparing minutes   **(2 marks)**

132 **The advantages of committees include which of the following?**

    A   Depth of consideration/Talent is pooled/Shared responsibilities/Delegation of authority

    B   Delegation of authority/Blurring responsibility and securing delay/Networking opportunities

    C   Shared responsibilities/Improves co-ordination/Valuable experience for fast tracked staff

    D   Responsibilities shared/More work undertaken/Delegation of authority/Decisions based on group assessment   **(2 marks)**

133 **As a requirement of the Combined Code of Corporate Governance, the remuneration committee of a large company determines the rates of pay and grades for all of the company's staff.**

    Is this statement true or false?   **(1 mark)**

134 **To be successful a committee should:**

    A   have clear terms of reference/have the necessary skills and experience/limit the number of members to, say, 10

    B   be cost-effective/frequently change its goals/Issue the agenda in advance

    C   circulate reports before a meeting/be cost-effective/be representative of all interests

    D   choose suitable subjects for action/have a written purpose/meet at least once a month.   **(2 marks)**

135 **The rules of procedure are designed for a number of purposes, including helping to minimise the effect of bullying tactics and ensuring that consistency and fair play are maintained.**

    Is this statement true or false?   **(2 marks)**

BUSINESS ETHICS AND BEHAVIOUR

136 When a company is following not only the letter, but the spirit of the law, it is said to:

    A   adopt a compliance-based approach to ethics

    B   adopt an integrity-based approach to ethics

    C   meet its social obligations

    D   follow the industry ethical code   **(2 marks)**

137 ACCA members are required to comply with five Fundamental Principles. Which of the following contains three of these principles?

    A   Integrity, Objectivity, (Honesty) ~not principle.~

    B   Professional competence and due care, Professional behaviour, Confidentiality

    C   Social responsibility, Independence, Scepticism

    D   Courtesy, Reliability, Responsibility   **(2 marks)**

138 All ACCA members must comply with the Fundamental Principles, whether or not they are in practice.

Is this statement true or false?   **(1 mark)**

139 Which of the following is an ethical proposition?

    A   Crime is increasing in the UK

    B   UK prison sentences should be as long as those in the US

    C   Most UK citizens believe that people are less honest than they used to be

    D   More murders are committed in London than in other UK city   **(2 marks)**

140 Some commentators stress that professionals owe an obligation to society above their duty to their client.

Is this statement true or false?   **(1 mark)**

141 Why does the professional accountant have a special role in promoting ethical behaviour throughout the business?

    A   S/he is seen as the guardian of the finances of the business

    B   They have undergone a lengthy period of study

    C   Ethics is often linked with financial probity

    D   Often s/he is the only person at meetings or on a board that belongs to a profession   **(2 marks)**

142   In which of the following situations would the company be viewed as having behaved unethically?

    A   Delaying payments to its suppliers despite continuous request

    B   Printing warning signs on its potentially dangerous plastic packaging

    C   Informing investors that the profit forecast may not materialise

    D   Stating that it will aim to recruit more people from ethnic minority groups   **(2 marks)**

143   Breaches of the ACCA Code of Ethics by ACCA members can result in their exclusion from membership.

    Is this statement true or false?   **(1 mark)**

GOVERNANCE AND SOCIAL RESPONSIBILITY

144   A UK oil company that judges that its shareholders' best interests are served by minimising its expenditure on measures to ensure that its plant and pipelines do not damage the environment is likely to be:

    A   applauded by major investors in the company

    B   criticised by major investors in the company

    C   supported by the media

    D   supported by the UK government   **(2 marks)**

145   Where there are a large number of external shareholders who play no role in the day-to-day running of a company, there is a situation that is described as:

    A   detached corporate ownership

    B   uninvolved external ownership

    C   dividend based shareholding

    D   separation of ownership and control   **(2 marks)**

146   The 'agency problem' refers to which of the following situations?

    A   Shareholders acting in their own short-term interests rather than the long-term interests of the company

    B   A vocal minority of shareholders expecting the directors to act as their agents and pay substantial dividends

    C   Companies reliant upon substantial government contracts such that they are effectively agents of the government

    D   The directors acting in their own interests rather than the shareholders' interests

    (2 marks)

147 **To encourage Executive Directors to operate in the best interests of the company, they could:**

A   be given a high basic salary

B   receive bonuses based on both individual and company's performance

C   be entitled to large payment on resignation

D   be asked to attend AGMs   **(2 marks)**

148 **Key issues in the corporate governance debate include:**

A   role of internal & external audit/size of dividend payments to shareholders

B   merits of 'going green'/need for governance legislation

C   deciding & disclosing directors' remuneration/calculation of directors' bonuses

D   role of internal & external audit/deciding & disclosing directors' remuneration

                                                                                (2 marks)

149 **Corporate social responsibility refers to the idea that a company should:**

A   play an active part in the social life of the local neighbourhood

B   be sensitive to the needs of all stakeholders

C   be alert to the social needs of all employees

D   act responsibly in relation to shareholders' overall needs – not just their financial
     needs   **(2 marks)**

150 **Which of the following would best explain the concept of sustainable development:**

A   starting business on the developed countries where the economic climate is conducive
     to trade

B   development which meets the needs of the present without compromising the ability
     of future generations to meet their own needs

C   sustaining the production at the level of maximum capacity

D   developing the business by signing long-term contracts with suppliers   **(2 marks)**

151 **Modern view on Corporate Social Responsibility is:**

A   it is a way to further a company's business and attract additional shareholders

B   it is necessary to reduce product liability claims

C   a company must give part of its profits to charity

D   social responsibility is incompatible with the objective of maximising shareholder's
     wealth   **(2 marks)**

152 **Balance scorecard approach to setting objectives emphasises:**

A   the importance of profitability above all other goals

B   the need to consider the customer expectations

C   the importance of setting a variety of goals to address different aspects of a company's
     performance

D   that investment in new products will decrease dividend available to shareholders

                                                                                (2 marks)

153 **Which of the following would render a non-executive director of a company unsuitable for this post?**

A   The person has enough time to carrying out the duties

B   The person is financially independent of the remuneration received for this post

C   He/she is employed part-time by the compnay and runs his/hers own company at the same time

D   The person owns a large number of the company's shares   **(2 marks)**

154 **A director should be involved in deciding the level of his / her remuneration so that his/ her views can be taken into account.**

Is this statement true or false?   **(1 mark)**

155 **One of the major problems that potentially reduce the effectiveness of internal auditors is:**

A   they are often unqualified

B   major companies have far flung subsidiaries all over the world

C   they are often significantly younger than board members

D   a board can underfund them   **(2 marks)**

156 **An audit committee should:**

A   comprise at least three NEDs

B   include at least one senior member of the internal audit team

C   include one member from the external audit firm

D   carry out a detailed review of critical elements of the balance sheet   **(2 marks)**

157 **The most obvious means of achieving public oversight of corporate governance is via:**

A   the company establishing a comprehensive web site

B   publication of the Annual Report and Accounts

C   press announcements of all significant developments

D   shareholder access to the Annual General Meeting   **(2 marks)**

LAW AND REGULATION GOVERNING ACCOUNTING

158 **When submitting annual financial statements to be available for inspection by third parties, a company should send them to:**

A   Stock exchange

B   Tax authorities

C   Shareholders

D   Companies house   **(2 marks)**

159 As there is no prescriptive definition of 'true and fair', it is implied that the financial statements must be properly repaired in accordance with accounting standards, follow generally accepted accounting practices and are not misleading.

Is this statement true or false?   **(1 mark)**

160 In order to prepare true and fair financial statements companies have to maintain 'proper accounting records'. How are 'proper accounting records' defined?

A   Records which are sufficient to enable the auditors to determine whether a true and fair view is shown by the financial statements

B   Records which are consistent with the reasonable needs of the company, its auditors and HMRC

C   They are not defined in law but set out in a number of Financial Reporting Standards (FRSs) which, in summary, require the company to maintain such records as will enable the company to produce financial statements that are in compliance with all the relevant FRSs

D   They are not defined but a record of transactions, assets and liabilities would be required as a minimum   **(2 marks)**

161 Failure to maintain proper accounting records is:

A   a criminal offence

B   both a civil and a criminal offence

C   neither a civil nor a criminal offence

D   a civil offence   **(2 marks)**

162 A qualified audit report means that the financial statements:

A   contain an element of fraud

B   are not entirely accurate

C   have not been approved by the Finance Director

D   do not give a true and fair view   **(2 marks)**

163 The key aim of the IASB (formerly the IASC) is to:

A   Improve the standards of financial reporting worldwide

B   Develop worldwide auditing standards

C   Harmonise accounting practice throughout the world

D   Represent UK interests effectively in financial reporting matters   **(2 marks)**

164 The role of IFRIC is to:

A   produce international accounting standards

B   supervise the development of international standards and guidance and help to raise money

C   advise the IASB as to which areas require new or amended standards

D   give guidance on (often topical) issues not covered in an accounting standard or where guidance is conflicting   **(2 marks)**

THE ACCOUNTING PROFESSION

165   When making a sales forecast for the forthcoming year, the Financial director is likely to consider both financial information, such as current year sales, and a non-financial information, such as the strength of competitive rivalry in the market.

Is this statement true or false?   **(1 mark)**

166   The predominant form of business entity is:

A   quoted companies

B   sole traders and partnerships

C   limited liability partnerships

D   limited liability companies   **(2 marks)**

167   The need for independent audit of financial statements arises because:

A   shareholders are not willing to spend time on analysing the financial statement

B   financial performance is nowadays seen as secondary to other organisational objectives

C   there is a separation of ownership and control

D   shareholders do not wish to interact with managers regarding company's performance
                                                                                (2 marks)

168   Luca Pacioli was the first person to introduce the idea of accountancy into business operations.

Is this statement true or false?   **(1 mark)**

169   The purpose of the accounting function is to:

A   advise management on the state of assets and liabilities

B   maintain comprehensive records of all transactions

C   produce information for internal and external stakeholders

D   produce information for decision-making purposes   **(2 marks)**

ACCOUNTING AND FINANCE FUNCTIONS

170   In a very large company working capital management would probably be the responsibility of the:

A   Finance director

B   Chief accountant

C   Treasurer

D   Management accountant   **(2 marks)**

171 Deciding which products or services to produce is usually part of:

    A   operational planning

    B   strategic planning

    C   production planning

    D   product planning   **(2 marks)**

172 The main financial statements produced each year are:

    A   Balance Sheet/Income statement/Annual report and accounts

    B   Profit forecasts/Balance Sheet/Annual report and accounts

    C   Profit warnings to the Stock Exchange/Balance Sheet/Income statement

    D   Cash flow statement/Balance Sheet/Income statement   **(2 marks)**

173 A is a small owner-managed company employing 20 staff and having a revenue of 300,000 Euro a year. It decided not to appoint external auditors to review its financial statement. Such a decision:

    A   is in line with the requirements of current legislations

    B   will be criticised by governmental authorities

    C   is likely to exacerbate the agency problem

    D   will allow the company to strengthen its financial controls   **(2 marks)**

174 Which of the following would be classed as a book of prime entry:

    A   Bank statement

    B   Trial balance

    C   Receivables ledger

    D   Income statement   **(2 marks)**

175 Which of the following methods of investment appraisal would allow assessment of how to minimise the risk caused by the long duration of aproject?

    A   Return on investment

    B   Expenditure budgeting

    C   Calculating the rate of return

    D   Break-even analysis   **(2 marks)**

176 S decided to record the purchases made on the 2nd of April 200X in tax year ending 31st of March 200X. This will be classed as tax avoidance by appropriate authorities.

Is this statement true or false?   **(1 mark)**

177 **Tax mitigation involves which of the following?**

A   Taking all legal steps to reduce one's tax liability

B   Agreeing to pay a financial penalty to avoid prosecution

C   Moving businesses and funds offshore to reduce liability to UK tax

D   Reducing tax liabilities without frustrating the law makers' intentions   **(2 marks)**

178 **An important advantage of using loans to finance investment is:**

A   loan interest payments can usually be suspended if profits are low

B   the timing of loan payments is often at the company's discretion

C   loan interest is tax deductible

D   banks will often not require security for loan advances   **(2 marks)**

179 **Working capital is calculated as:**

A   the excess of current assets over current liabilities

B   the excess of bank borrowings over current assets

C   the excess of long -term liabilities over short-term liabilities

D   the excess of fixed assets over current assets   **(2 marks)**

FINANCIAL SYSTEMS AND PROCEDURES

180 **To make sure that an inventory check is effective which of the following needs to be done?**

A   One person is to count all the items

B   Appropriate notice is to be issued before an inventory check visit is due

C   Inventory check report is signed by a warehouse representative only

D   There should be a systematic approach to counting the items   **(2 marks)**

181 **Which of the following actions is most likely to prevent damage to goods during handling?**

A   Putting them into transparent plastic boxes

B   Training staff on handling procedures

C   Only storing goods that are durable

D   Outsourcing inventory handling to an external supplier   **(2 marks)**

182 **Credit notes are normally issued when:**

A   the customer has overpaid

B   there is a credit balance on the supplier's account

C   an accountant has put a reminder to record a journal crediting receivables

D   a due discount was not applied to an invoice sent to the customer   **(2 marks)**

183 One of the disadvantages of having formal written procedures for recording transactions is that fraud and errors are more difficult to detect.

Is this statement true or false? **(1 mark)**

184 Analysis of revenue and expenses often involves use of unique code numbers so that income and expenditure can be recorded by:

A type and department

B date and staff involved

C purchaser and supplier

D the particular company within a group that is involved **(2 marks)**

185 Which of the following would ensure that the sales cycle results in prompt payment?

A Orders are processed by qualified personnel only

B Checking the goods are in inventory before dispatching them

C Each item has its own code

D Checking the creditworthiness of the customer **(2 marks)**

186 The most secure and easy to verify way to pay staff is by:

A sending company checks

B using BACS transfers

C paying people in cash

D asking staff to visit the accounts office to receive their wages **(2 marks)**

187 To add security to the process, cheques issued for a large amount of money will often involve:

A a faster clearing process at the bank

B the approval of a senior member of the accounts department

C two signatories

D automated checks on signatures **(2 marks)**

188 When petty cash is replenished, it is usual for the amount of cash to drawn to equal the value of the receipts and vouchers produced since the previous replenishment.

Is this statement true or false? **(1 mark)**

189 The incidence of fraud indicates a weakness in:

A security arrangements

B system procedures

C recruitment procedures

D organisational control **(2 marks)**

190   A company that predominantly receives cheques and postal orders in payment for goods dispatched should appoint a designated and trusted individual to open the mail.

Is this statement true or false?   **(1 mark)**

191   'Ghost' employees:

A   vanish when demanding tasks are allocated

B   take an excessive amount of time off work

C   impersonate other employees to gain a financial advantage

D   are paid a salary but do not work for the company   **(2 marks)**

192   Which of the following is an advantage of manual systems?

A   They have fewer errors than automated systems

B   They are easier to audit than automated systems

C   It is easier to correct errors than in automated systems

D   They are more secure than automated systems   **(2 marks)**

THE RELATIONSHIP OF ACCOUNTING WITH OTHER BUSINESS FUNCTIONS

193   What is the key role of the accounting department in relation to prices paid for goods purchased?

A   To advise on comparable prices elsewhere

B   To advise on the reliability of the supplier

C   To ensure that the purchases budget is not exceeded

D   To maintain margins   **(2 marks)**

194   Despite the different primary nature of their work, Accounts and IT department representatives could both be members of a Steering Committee.

Is this statement true or false?   **(1 mark)**

195   A company with a marketing orientation believes that:

A   products should be sold actively and aggressively

B   meeting customer needs better than competitors is the key to corporate success

C   the level of sales, advertising and sales promotion is key to corporate success

D   producing goods and services of optimum quality is the key to corporate success
                                                                  (2 marks)

196   The marketing mix is best described as:

A   a team of people from the marketing department who are in charge of reviewing the company's product selection

B   the marketing department in transition

C   greater emphasis on marketing than sales

D   a set of variables blended to produce desired results   **(2 marks)**

197   In the context of the evaluation of the marketing mix, which of the following are the two main product issues to consider?

A   Price and Presentation

B   Place and Promotion

C   Definition and Positioning

D   Quality and Price   **(2 marks)**

198   Which of the following pricing strategies is aimed at gaining market share?

A   Penetration pricing

B   Going rate pricing

C   Price skimming

D   Loss leaders   **(2 marks)**

199   Captive product pricing describes a pricing strategy where:

A   prices are substantially increased shortly after the product launch

B   the product or service is available from only one supplier

C   customers must buy two products

D   the product is expected to fail frequently, necessitating further purchases   **(2 marks)**

200   The key decision under 'place' when reviewing the marketing mix is whether to sell direct or to sell indirect.

Is this statement true or false?   **(1 mark)**

201   The strategic marketing process has three strategic elements:

A   analysis/implementation/review

B   research/choice/implementation

C   research/resolution/review

D   analysis/choice/implementation   **(2 marks)**

202   **Market research carried out as part of the strategic planning process will typically fall under which of the following headings?**

    A   Internal research, External research, Test trials

    B   Corporate research, Personal research, Trial launch

    C   In house research, Ground research, Field trials

    D   Desk research, Field research, Test marketing   **(2 marks)**

203   **When considering the sequence in which marketing activities take place, targeting is done first followed by market segmentation.**

    Is this statement true or false?   **(1 mark)**

INTERNAL AND EXTERNAL AUDIT

204   **The key purpose of internal auditing is to:**

    A   detect errors and fraud

    B   evaluate the organisation's risk management processes and systems of control

    C   give confidence as to the truth and fairness of the financial statements

    D   express an internal opinion on the truth and fairness of the financial statements   **(2 marks)**

205   **Internal auditors can be company employees or a firm of accountants.**

    Is this statement true or false?   **(1 mark)**

206   **The Combined Code on Corporate Governance states that companies without an internal audit function should review the need for one:**

    A   every year

    B   every two years

    C   every five years

    D   every ten years   **(2 marks)**

207   **Internal auditors have an unavoidable .... problem.**

    Which word correctly completes this sentence?

    A   Integrity

    B   Independence

    C   Loyalty   **(1 mark)**

208   **It is the considered to be best practice for the internal auditors of a large company to report to:**

    A   the board of directors

    B   the external auditors

    C   the shareholders

    D   the audit committee

209 If internal auditors identify fraud why might they be unwilling to disclose it?

    A   The fraud could have been perpetrated by an internal auditor

    B   Disclosure could result in adverse personal consequences for the internal auditors

    C   Disclosure could reflect badly on the quality of their previous internal audit work

    D   Disclosure would spoil their chances of benefiting from the fraud   **(2 marks)**

210 Substantive testing means that the external auditor will check the extent to which the internal controls could be relied on

Is this statement true or false?   **(1 mark)**

211 Companies listed on the London Stock Exchange are legally bound to appoint internal auditors and to resource them appropriately.

Is this statement true or false?   **(1 mark)**

212 There is greater flexibility in how internal audit work is done relative to external audit work, since external audit work is controlled by the law and audit standards.

Is this statement true or false?   **(1 mark)**

213 To practice as an internal auditor, the person must be ACCA qualified.

Is this statement true or false?   **(1 mark)**

INTERNAL FINANCIAL CONTROL

214 The fact that managers are not aware of problems a company is facing, such as not knowing that a major incident of fraud has recently taken place, would weaken which of the following components of internal controls?

    A   Control environment

    B   Risk assessment process

    C   Control activities

    D   Monitoring of controls

    (2 marks)

215 The amount of substantive testing of transactions and resultant balances carried out by the external auditors should be most influenced by which of the following?

    A   The quality of the relationship between the external auditors and the internal auditors

    B   The qualifications and experience of the internal auditors

    C   The quality of the internal controls

    D   The organisation's ability to afford the resulting audit fee

    (2 marks)

216 Which of the following controls would be most effective when processing customer refunds?

A   Segregation of duties

B   Authorisation

C   Reconciliation

D   Maintaining a trial balance

(2 marks)

217 When considering computer controls, the company that encourages their staff to use the same login details when using their accounting package would be classed as having sufficiently high level of controls.

Is this statement true or false? **(1 mark)**

218 A requirement that no one person should have the ability to make payments to payables and write up the purchase ledger is an example of the important general principle known as:

A   controlled record access

B   segregation of duties

C   dual control

D   initiation control **(2 marks)**

219 The Auditing Practices Board defines internal control as being concerned with providing reasonable assurance as to the achievement of the entity's objectives with regard to which of the following?

A   The reasonableness of directors' remuneration

B   Reliability of financial reporting

C   Minimisation of errors and fraud

D   The financial statements showing a true and fair view **(2 marks)**

220 Internal check is an element of internal control, concerned with ensuring that no single task is executed from start to finish ....

Which of the following accurately complete this sentence?

A   by fewer than three people

B   unsupervised

C   by only one person **(1 mark)**

221 The level and extent of internal controls required depends on which of the following?

A   The value of the assets at risk

B   What the risks are if such controls fail

C   The significance to the organisation of the operations to which the internal controls are being applied

D   The level of uncovered insurance exposure associated with the activity in question. **(2 marks)**

222 Which of the following would be classed as a preventive control?

    A   Having a supervisor present on the shop floor at all times

    B   Conducting regular receivables statement reconciliations

    C   Weekly inventory checks

    D   Establishing procedures for irrecoverable debt collection   **(2 marks)**

223 Internal auditors need to be adding value and therefore will review the cost effectiveness as well as the adequacy of controls.

Is this statement true or false?   **(1 mark)**

224 Business risk is the possibility that an event or transaction could occur that will adversely affect the organisation's ability to:

    A   achieve its objectives and execute its strategies

    B   continue in existence in its present form

    C   realise its economic targets in the short and medium term

    D   provide product or customer service to a level acceptable to its customers   **(2 marks)**

225 Every evening the last person leaving the office premises needs to switch on the security alarm. This control belongs to which of the following categories?

    A   Authorisation

    B   Computer

    C   Reconciliation

    D   Physical   **(2 marks)**

226 Who is responsible for the company's system of internal control?

    A   The Finance Director

    B   The internal auditors

    C   The board of directors

    D   The external auditors   **(1 mark)**

FRAUD

227 The three prerequisites for fraud to occur are motive, opportunity and weak controls.

Is this statement true or false?   **(1 mark)**

228 Which of the following is a skimming fraud?

    A   A large amount is 'skimmed' off the top of a large sales invoice as a kickback to the purchaser

    B   Small amounts are diverted from a large number of transactions

    C   Invitation to pay a large amount up front to secure a large amount in the future

    D   Submission of invoices which contain inflated amounts   **(2 marks)**

229 'Teeming and lading' is used to describe which of the following:

    A   Where money flows are so substantial that diversion of large sums can go unnoticed

    B   A fraud where purchase ledger payments are misdirected to overseas accounts

    C   A personal expenses fraud involving fictitious expense vouchers

    D   A fraud where receipts from customers are misappropriated   **(2 marks)**

230 'Window dressing' involves which of the following:

    A   Producing a lavishly illustrated set of annual accounts in years when underlying results are poor

    B   Entering into transactions before the year end that will improve the appearance of the accounts

    C   Presenting an asset or a transaction in a flattering and deceptive light

    D   Inflation of sales volumes by retailers   **(2 marks)**

231 Off balance sheet accounting refers to which of the following:

    A   A focus on income and expenditure rather to the detriment of asset and liability management

    B   Fraudulent concealment of a liability

    C   Diversion of assets from the balance sheet to a personal bank account

    D   Deliberate exclusion of certain assets and liabilities from the published balance sheet   **(2 marks)**

232 A comprehensive system of control will eliminate all fraud and error.

    Is this statement true or false?   **(1 mark)**

233 Employees working in departments other than Accounts have no responsibility for reporting fraud.

    Is this statement true or false?   **(1 mark)**

234 If an external auditor in the process of considering the company's financial statement came across an incident of fraud that took place in the year, he/she must qualify company's accounts.

    Is this statement true or false?   **(1 mark)**

235 Which of the following behaviours is often associated with an employee possibly committing fraud?

    A   Managers and staff having monthly meetings to discuss underperformance

    B   Employee frequently taking time off work for personal reasons

    C   A member of the Finance team frequently buying new expensive cars despite only earning a moderate salary

    D   Member of HR team being keen to take part in discussion on staff remuneration

    (2 marks)

RECRUITMENT AND SELECTION, MANAGING DIVERSITY AND EQUAL OPPORTUNITY

236 When an applicant first comes into contact with an organisation, a prime source of dissatisfaction is often:

A   the number of interviews before a decision is made

B   the nature of the questions posed at interview

C   the failure to recompense the applicant for his/her travel expenses

D   the high level of expectations resulting from the job advertisement   **(2 marks)**

237 When an organisation needs to recruit for a specific skill, applicants are likely to be best reached through which of the following media?

A   National press

B   Radio and TV

C   The Internet

D   Trade, technical or professional journals   **(2 marks)**

238 A document containing skills and knowledge expected of staff occupying a certain position is referred to as:

A   job description

B   personal specification

C   job evaluation

D   job specification   **(2 marks)**

239 Recruitment consultants are often particularly useful when it comes to identifying which of the short-listed candidates should get the job.

Is this statement true or false?   **(1 mark)**

240 Economic uncertainty has the effect of .... the number of job applicants.

Which word correctly completes this sentence?

A   Reducing

B   Increasing

C   Multiplying   **(1 mark)**

241 A job description is a statement of:

A   the positioning of the role within the organisation overall and the relevant work area

B   the key requirements of the employer mapped against the attributes of the ideal candidate

C   the terms and conditions of employment relative that apply to a particular job

D   the purpose, scope, duties and responsibilities of the job   **(2 marks)**

242 In practice when sending a reference request for a new employee and asking to comment on whether this person is a worthy member of staff, the company:

    A   will receive a response outlining every detail of the person's past performance

    B   will be asked to send another request outlining what criteria constitute trustworthiness

    C   will receive a response containing the person's position and employment dates

    D   Will be in breach of employment legislations   **(2 marks)**

243 A selection interview not only aims to help choose the best person for the job but also to make the candidates feel that they have been fairly treated in the process.

Is this statement true or false?   **(1 mark)**

244 The concept of diversity embodies the belief that people should be:

    A   treated with respect regardless of their age, ethnicity or background

    B   encouraged to develop the cultural activities associated with their country of origin

    C   encouraged to adopt the way of life of their own cultural group

    D   valued for their difference and variety   **(2 marks)**

245 In the context of diversity, what should management seek to achieve in relation to its operational environment?

    A   Equal opportunity for all staff to flourish in that environment

    B   A workforce that is representative of that environment

    C   Active participation by staff in that operational environment

    D   Nothing – the operational environment is not relevant to diversity   **(2 marks)**

246 Which of the following types of equal opportunities legislation typically prohibits discrimination on the basis of marital status or gender?

    A   Rehabilitation of offenders

    B   Sex discrimination

    C   Age discriminations

    D   Race relations   **(2 marks)**

247 'Halo' effect in the selection process refers to:

    A   people possessing supernatural skills

    B   an employee being a very strong leader

    C   a judgement being based on first impressions

    D   employing a person with strong religious persuasion   **(2 marks)**

248 When many candidates need to be assessed at the same time using a variety of interacting techniques, the company is likely to use:

A   panel interviews

B   personality tests

C   application forms

D   assessment centre   **(2 marks)**

249 Which of the following would ensure that there is a firm commitment on a candidate's behalf to accept the position?

A   Inviting candidates for an office visit, so they can see how the company operates

B   Calling back the preferred candidate to verify the length of his/hers notice period

C   Receiving a signed employment contract

D   Receiving a signed application form   **(2 marks)**

250 Induction process is:

A   a presentation done for a new and highly important customer

B   an introductory product offer being made available for a limited time

C   the process when staff are asked to participate in simulation of a customer-related situation

D   the process of settling a new recruit into the organisation   **(2 marks)**

REVIEW AND APPRAISAL OF INDIVIDUAL PERFORMANCE

251 When considering the criteria which should be used to assess employee performance, a manager should take into account:

A   how the company has performed over the last year

B   the number of times the employee has not attended staff parties

C   the volume and quality of work done by the employee

D   how frequently the employee has requested to take holidays   **(2 marks)**

252 The three types of staff appraisal process are included in which of the following:

A   inward and outward looking/management of objectives/task centred method

B   review and comparison/management by objectives/task centred method

C   results oriented method/forward and backward review management by exception

D   people oriented method/results oriented method/management by objectives **(2 marks)**

253 When asking an employee to fill in the self-appraisal form, a manager often means that this information is only required for good recordkeeping.

Is this statement true or false?   **(1 mark)**

254   Effective appraisal is grounded in the belief that:

   A   a review of the past and a plan for the future is good management

   B   identification and agreement of both strengths and weaknesses is key to personal advancement

   C   an open and two-way review of performance is valuable to both the appraisee and appraiser

   D   feedback on past performance influences future performance   **(2 marks)**

255   The reasons for staff leaving fall into three categories: Discharge, Unavoidable and Avoidable.

   Is this statement true or false?   **(1 mark)**

256   Conducting an appraisal in a public place, such as staff canteen, may render it ineffective because of:

   A   lack of objective judgement

   B   problems of confidentiality

   C   there is no time to fill in appropriate paperwork

   D   it will be effective as other members of staff could overhear the conversation and contribute their views   **(2 marks)**

257   Performance appraisal could be seen as a part of company's succession planning strategy.

   Is this statement true or false?   **(1 mark)**

258   Staff turnover can be calculated by dividing either the total number leaving the organisation, or the total replacements, by the number in the workforce and expressing the result as a percentage.

   Is this statement true or false?   **(1 mark)**

TRAINING DEVELOPMENT AND LEARNING

259   Which of the following training methods would be suitable for a trainee accountant seeking a professional qualification and a till operator who is moving to a new machine?

   A   Computer based training/Evening classes

   B   Evening classes/On-the-job training

   C   Day release/External course

   D   Self-managed learning/Coaching   **(2 marks)**

260   Learning can be defined as 'the process of acquiring knowledge through experience, which leads to a change in .... '.

   Which word correctly completes this sentence?

   A   Perception

   B   Understanding

   C   Behaviour   **(1 mark)**

261 The pace of learning or progress changes with ....

Which word correctly completes this sentence?

A   Familiarity

B   The type of task in question

C   One's confidence level   **(1 mark)**

262 Kolb has suggested that there are four stages in the learning process and it is most productive to start with experience stage.

Is this statement true or false?   **(1 mark)**

263 Many management writers have said that if you want to develop an organisation then develop its people and they will develop the organisation.

Is this statement true or false?   **(1 mark)**

264 Providing employees with continuing professional development (CPD) opportunities – as the title implies – involves an ongoing commitment to develop professional skills and the potential time and cost involved for both the organisation and the individual are such that CPD should be confined to professional staff or managers.

Is this statement true or false?   **(1 mark)**

265 Which of the following learning styles is best adjusted to acquiring knowledge from group interaction and team work?

A   Activist

B   Reflectors

C   Theories

D   Pragmatist   **(2 marks)**

266 An important implication of Kolb and Honey and Mumford's theories is that people will tend to learn more effectively if:

A   learning involves a significant amount of repetition

B   learning is geared to their preferred learning style

C   learning is supported by an enthusiastic teacher

D   learning appears to offer tangible practical benefits   **(2 marks)**

267 A training 'gap' is any surplus of knowledge, understanding, skill or attitudes, measured against what is required by the job or the demands of organisational change.

Is this statement true or false?   **(1 mark)**

268 Which of the following approaches to development is most similar to succession planning?

A   Management development

B   Coaching

C   CPD

D   Personal development   **(2 marks)**

269   The role of management in a learning organisation is to encourage:

A   continuous learning and acquisition of new knowledge and skills

B   job-based learning and skills acquisition

C   the development and use of a knowledge and skills database

D   a structured and methodical approach to knowledge and skill acquisition   **(2 marks)**

270   Mentoring process refers to a trainee following a more experienced member of staff, trying to pick up what he/she does through observation and repetition.

Is this statement true or false?   **(1 mark)**

271   Hamblin's five levels of training evaluation do not include an attempt to measure how the organisation as a whole has benefited from the training – the evaluation is confined to the training's impact at the individual and departmental level.

Is this statement true or false?   **(1 mark)**

IMPROVING PERSONAL EFFECTIVENESS AT WORK

272   Relative to training, personal development is more general forward-looking, orientated towards the individual and concerned with fulfilling the individual's potential.

Is this statement true or false?   **(1 mark)**

273   Which of the following is unlikely to be a goal of a personal development plan?

A   Growth during person's career

B   Meeting weekly sales targets

C   Developing skills and expertise

D   Realising personal aspiration   **(2 marks)**

274   The stages of preparing a personal development plan are contained in which of the following?

A   Position analysis/Attributes/Objectives

B   Past successes & failures/Corrective action/Review

C   Objectives / Detailed plan/Review

D   SWOT analysis/Setting goals/Action plan   **(2 marks)**

275   Two important time management techniques are included in which of the following?

A   Learning from others/Working with good time managers

B   Producing an activity log/Making lists

C   Prioritising/Charging out your time

D   'Borrowing' time/Planning and organising   **(2 marks)**

276 As a tool to improve time management skills, a person may try to calculate one's opportunity costs. This will include:

A   considering what impact it will have if things were to be done later rather than now

B   taking an opportunity to do nothing while the manager is away

C   looking at how much time could be made free by completing the project to set deadlines

D   considering how to make the jobs last longer in order to increase pay when on an hourly rate **(2 marks)**

277 Counselling normally deals with issues such as lack of experience or technical knowledge necessary to fulfil the job requirements.

Is this statement true or false? **(1 mark**

278 Which of the following contains two of the three core objectives of the mentoring process?

A   Knowledge transfer/Measurable results

B   Ongoing relationship/Tangible benefits

C   Measurable outcomes/Holistic growth

D   Exchange of knowledge/Sustained partnering relationship **(2 marks)**

279 During the counselling sessions, the counsellor is likely to set the concrete goals that the individual needs to achieve before coming back for the next session.

Is this statement true or false? **(1 mark)**

280 The four generations of time management approaches outlined by Stephen Covey are: Reminders; Planning and preparation; Planning, prioritising and controlling; Being efficient and proactive.

Is this statement true or false? **(1 mark)**

281 Personal effectiveness is best described as:

A   managing one's time efficiently

B   achieving results quickly

C   securing objectives without trampling on people

D   setting the right goals and objectives and then securing them **(2 marks)**

EFFECTIVE COMMUNICATION AND INTERPERSONAL SKILLS

282 Grapevine communication network is often used by managers to pass on orders and instruction to staff.

Is this statement true or false? **(1 mark)**

283 **Communication is best described as:**

A   the interchange of information, ideas, etc

B   the message

C   what is received by the recipient

D   clear expression   **(2 marks)**

284 **When communicating with others, the majority of information passed on to the other person is transmitted through words rather than other means such as body language or tone of voice.**

Is this statement true or false?   **(1 mark)**

285 **The use of predetermined lists of recipients for instructions, control reports, etc often results in some of the recipients investigating matters which have no relevance to the job they do.**

Is this true or false?   **(1 mark)**

286 **When there are significant barriers to communication it is important to:**

A   understand how the barriers came about

B   cancel the message that has not got through

C   ensure that the particular channel is not used again in the short term

D   identify the barriers and ways of dealing with them   **(2 marks)**

287 **Barriers to communication consist of anything that stops information getting to its intended recipients.**

Is this statement true or false?   **(1 mark)**

288 **Which of the following is an example of lateral communication?**

A   A manager explaining new operational procedures to staff

B   A committee coming together to review health and safety issues

C   Staff passing on to the supervisor the main points from a recent conversation with a customer

D   During appraisal, a person receives feedback about his performance results **(2 marks)**

289 **In the communication process the third stage is:**

A   encoding the message

B   receiving the message

C   selecting an appropriate medium

D   formulating a response   **(2 marks)**

290   The five popular patterns of communication can be split (according to the ways in which the information flows between users) into which of the following categories?

A   Centralised/Decentralised

B   Head office/Subsidiaries

C   National/International

D   Telecoms/Optical fibre   **(2 marks)**

291   Information overload usually leads to individual being unable to decide what information is relevant or not, and therefore important facts may be missed out.

Is this statement true or false?   **(1 mark)**

292   Research has shown that the level of satisfaction for individuals is lowest in the circle pattern of communication.

Is this statement true or false?   **(1 mark)**

293   Research on communication networks has shown that the quickest way to reach a conclusion is always through:

A   the Circle

B   the 'Y'

C   the wheel

D   the chain   **(2 marks)**

294   Under time pressure, the all-channels system either:

A   delivers even better results

B   partially closes down or disintegrates

C   slows down or crashes

D   restructures or disintegrates   **(2 marks)**

295   For complex problems the network most likely to facilitate the best decision is:

A   circle

B   all-channel

C   wheel

D   'Y'   **(2 marks)**

Section 2

ANSWERS TO PRACTICE QUESTIONS

THE BUSINESS ORGANISATION

1   C

A social responsibility objective allows the company to focus on the long-term survival and is often a part of the Ethical Code.

2   A

Education is the correct answer because the other organisations are normally found in the private sector.

3   C

C is the correct answer because this is the main activity in the public sector. Options A and B relate to the private sector and D to a mutual organisation.

4   FALSE

Publicly owned companies are usually run by the government.

5   C

C is the correct answer because the shareholders have limited liability – this means their liability is limited to the amount paid for the share capital.

6   C

Production is preoccupied with operations, Research and Development with innovation, and Purchasing with negotiating the most advantageous trading terms.

7   C

Co-operatives are organised solely to meet the needs of the member-owners. Ownership does not arise in the case of Schools and Councils; ownership and control are separate in the case of limited companies.

8   A

Standardisation of skills is achieved through staff training, standardisation of processes by adopting best work techniques and standardisation of output is necessary to ensure customer satisfaction.

9   D

The other two steps are Strategic analysis and Strategic implementation. A is part of Strategic choice, B is part of Strategic analysis and C is part of Strategic implementation.

10   C

The other two levels – which precede Operational planning – are Strategic planning and Tactical planning.

11   C

Organisations make people more powerful as there are more like-minded people around that will encourage the person to convert his ideas into real products.

12   A

Taylor believed in 'one best way' to organise the firm and do the individual job.

ORGANISATIONAL STRUCTURE

13   B

Entrepreneurial structure is built around the owner manager and is typical of small companies in the early stages of their development. The owner manager will often exercise direct control over all staff.

14   D

The informal organisation evolves over time and is a network of relationships within an organisation that arise due to common interests or friendships. The informal organisation can either enhance or hold back the business since it often embraces both advantages (e.g. higher levels of motivation) and disadvantages (e.g. opposition to change).

15   D

Function managers may make decisions to increase their own power, or in the interests of their own function, rather than in the interests of the company overall. Economies of scale, standardisation and specialists feeling comfortable are advantages of a functional structure.

16   C

A matrix structure aims to combine the benefits of decentralisation (e.g. speedy decision making) with those of co-ordination. The more rigid structure in a divisional company would not have the necessary flexibility.

17   FALSE

The scalar chain is the line of authority which can be traced up or down the chain of command, and thus relates to the number of management levels in an organisation.

18   C

Functional flexibility refers people being able to complete many of the organisational tasks

19   C

As people work together in teams, they also move frequently between different projects, thus each member of staff will accumulate a wide network of contacts.

20   D

The granting of authority over each geographic area to geographic bosses results in a potential loss of control over key operating decisions. This weakness is also present in the Product/Division/Department structure.

21   TRUE

The managers therefore rely on banks and the market (the owners) to provide the investment.

22   C

It makes it more difficult to manage staff remotely, therefore a manager is likely to look after fewer employees.

23   A

Better local decisions are likely due to local expertise. Other advantages are the freeing of senior management to concentrate on strategy, better motivation due to increased training and career path, and quicker responses.

ORGANISATIONAL CULTURE

24   FALSE

Handy expressed culture as 'the way we do things around here'.

25   TRUE

History of the organisation plays an important role in shaping the mindset of the employees as it creates examples for them to follow in the future.

26   B

Schein described these aspects of culture as artefacts. The other two levels are espoused values (strategies and goals, including slogans) and basic assumptions and values – these are difficult to identify as they are unseen, and exist mainly at the unconscious level.

27   C

The person culture exists to satisfy the personal requirements of the particular individuals involved in the organisation, e.g. a barrister. The other three cultural types are the power culture (one major source of power), the role culture (people describe their job by its duties, not its purpose) and the task culture (where task achievement is paramount).

28   B

Person culture focuses on the need of the few selected individuals who occupy the prominent place. A is compatible with the task culture, whereas C and D are common in role culture.

29   B

This is one of the five national traits identified by Hofstede. The other four traits are Individualism v Collectivism (some cultures are more cohesive); Power/distance (the extent to which cultures are prepared to accept an inferior position); Masculinity vFemininity (masculine role = big distinction between the roles of the genders, feminine role = differences between the gender roles much smaller) and Confucianism v dynamism (attitude to change over the long term).

LEADERSHIP, MANAGEMENT AND SUPERVISION

30   C

Contingency theory sees effective leadership as being dependent on a number of variable or contingent factors – in Adair's case these variables are task needs, individual needs and group needs. Adair's model looks at leadership in relation to the needs of the task, individual and group.

31   D

Psychologically distant leaders favour formal roles and relationships, judge subordinates on the basis of performance and are primarily task oriented. In contrast psychologically close leaders do not seek to formalise roles and relationships and are more concerned with maintaining good relationships at work. Their style works best when the situation is moderately favourable.

32   B

Heifetz suggested that adaptive change is required when the problem cannot be solved with existing skills and knowledge and requires people to make a shift in their values, expectations, attitudes or habits of behaviour. This is often required to ensure organisational survival.

33   C

A basic definition of a leader is 'someone who exercises influence over other people'. This can be expanded into the more complex definition above.

34   A

All managers have in common the overall aim of getting things done and delegating to other people rather than doing everything themselves.

35   C

This definition best captures the key elements of a supervisor's responsibilities, which are primarily concerned with planning and controlling the work of their group.

36   D

In return the organisation was obliged to provide job security and good remuneration. A is the view of Mayo and B and C are the view of Bennis.

37   A

The human relations approach suggests that relationship and interactions are more important to creating a productive workforce than money or imposed standards.

38   D

Contingency theorists do not ignore the lessons learnt from earlier theorists – they adapt them.

39   C

In Mintzberg's view, these are the ten skills managers need to develop greater effectiveness. The ten skills are as follows: **Interpersonal** – Figurehead, Leader, Liaison. **Informational** – Monitor, Disseminator, Spokesperson. **Decisional** – Entrepreneur, Disturbance handler, Resource allocator, Negotiator.

40   TRUE

Authority is thus another word for legitimate power.

41   D

Line authority runs down the vertical chain of command; Staff authority is the authority a manager or department may have in giving specialist advice; Functional authority is a hybrid of line and staff authority whereby a manager setting policies and procedures for the company as a whole has the authority to direct another department.

42   C

This is one of the strongest sources of power as people are influenced by it irrespectively of the manager's proximity and would voluntarily change their behaviour in a desirable way.

43   TRUE

As every employee is responsible for his/her area of work and is accountable to the superior. In the case of the Board of directors, they are responsible for the performance of the organisation as a whole and have to justify the result to the organisation's stakeholders such as shareholders.

44   B

Early studies of leadership were based on the assumption that leaders were born and not made. The physical traits included drive and energy; the Personality traits included adaptability and enthusiasm and the Social traits included co-operation and tact.

45   B

The grid measures concern for production on the horizontal axis and concern for people on the vertical axis. A 1.9 manager has the lowest production score on the horizontal axis (little work is achieved), but the highest people score on the vertical axis (the manager is attentive to the needs of people).

46   C

Tells = Autocratic; Sells = Persuasive; Consults = Participative; Joins = Democratic.

INDIVIDUAL AND GROUP BEHAVIOUR IN BUSINESS ORGANISATIONS

47   D

Role conflict refers to the situation when there is a clash between the roles, such as the role of the employee and role of good auditor.

48   D

Assertive behaviour is direct and professional; Aggressive behaviour violates another person's rights; Passive behaviour is giving in to another person.

49   D

The combined activity of separate entities has a greater effect than the sum of the activities of each entity working alone.

50   A

The other factors required for a cohesive group are a commitment to shared goals, team identity and team solidarity.

TEAM FORMATION, DEVELOPMENT AND MANAGEMENT

51   D

A, B and C are qualities of a Team.

52   TRUE

A team is a formal group that has a leader and a distinctive culture and is geared towards a final result.

53   C

Synergy and the use of specialists to deal with complex problems are the key ingredients of the basic purpose of a team.

54   A

The other six roles are Monitor-evaluator; Resource investigator; Company worker; Team worker; Finisher and Expert.

55   C

The plant role is played by a creative individual, the monitor-evaluator is good at making accurate judgements, whereas the team worker looks after the atmosphere within the team.

56   B

This is a conflict stage when people start to withdraw their cooperation and therefore jobs are not completed to the expected standard.

57   C

Dorming refers to the danger that the team will be operating on automatic pilot. Tuckman's first four stages are Forming; Storming; Norming and Performing.

MOTIVATING INDIVIDUALS AND GROUPS

58   C

According to Herzberg, working conditions are a hygiene factor or dissatisfier.

Working conditions, like a pay rise, can be a short-term motivator, but is unlikely to have a lasting effect.

59   C

The work of office staff is usually hard to quantify, however they have a significant influence on the income a company generates and therefore it is presumed that they should share a part of the profit.

60   TRUE

In the short run you can have one without the other, but in the long run there is usually congruence.

61   FALSE

Content theories focus on what motivates people, they consider that we are all driven by the same set of desires. Process theories encourage a manager to communicate with staff to establish what rewards are of value to them and whether the targets set are achievable and realistic.

62   B

This would meet the need for recognition and status.

63   C

Individuals may seek to satisfy a number of needs at the same time.

64   C

It allows people to grow personally and professionally by exposing them to higher levels of responsibility and more challenging tasks.

65   FALSE

This approach would be appropriate to Theory X workers, who must be coerced to get them to make an effort.

For Theory Y workers, a participative, liberating, developmental approach would be appropriate.

66   A

Such people are seen as lazy and will work only if there is a direct link between efforts and rewards.

67   C

As Theory X workers see their work as menial, putting them on piece rate is often the only way to motivate them.

68   D

Vroom's theory may be stated as Force = Valence x Expectancy.

69   FALSE

The statement describes intrinsic rewards. Extrinsic rewards are separate from (or external to) the job itself and are dependent upon the decisions of others, e.g. pay and benefits.

70   C

MBO means that an employee is given a range of targets he needs to achieve and the assessment is based on the degree of success in all the areas. Thus, many people may feel overstretched and find it difficult to prioritise.

INFORMATION TECHNOLOGY AND INFORMATION SYSTEMS IN BUSINESS

71   FALSE

Intranet is only accessible be people within the company. An extranet could give access to selected parties to enable them to view some of the company's information.

72   A

Information is different from data – which is not in a form suitable for making decisions.

73   D

Computers made it easier to record, store, analyse and present the information.

74   C

The mnemonic to remember is **ACCURATE** and the other four qualities are **C**ost (relative to the benefits), **A**daptable, **T**imely and **E**asy to use.

75   D

An organisation's information systems must be organised in such a way as to meet the information needs of these various levels of management.

76   B

Database systems are the organisation's memory. Enquiry systems provide specific information and support systems facilitate analysis, forecasts and simulations.

77   D

An internal source means that this information is already in existence within the organisation. A, B and C are all external sources.

78   C

These systems are used for routine tasks in which data items or transactions must be processed so that operations can continue.

79   D

A MIS might, for example, generate reports on total sales for each item using data from a transaction processing system.

80   C

This system can make decisions independently based on the predetermined criteria. It is also frequently used for giving recommendations in areas such as banking, medicine and law.

81   A

If there is a programme bug or a virus that affected the database, it often means that the whole storage is affected and the entire set of data will be lost.

82   B

In some ways EIS resemble, in outcomes, Decision Support Systems, (DSS), but whereas the DSS provides tools that require significant expertise to use, the EIS is designed to help managers find the information they need easily and in the most appropriate format.

POLITICAL AND LEGAL FACTORS

83   C

A = Technological heading, B = Economic heading, D = Social heading.

84   TRUE

As with all external analysis, the factors presented may present firms with opportunities or threats.

85   A

Lobbying is often associated with actions taken by individuals or organisations in an attempt to influence the policy-making process.

86   FALSE

Privatisation refers to a government selling its assets.

87   D

All firms also have to comply with health and safety and data protection legislation.

88   A

Other sources include the International Court of Justice, European parliament, European courts and certain international agreements, e.g. World Trade Organisation rules.

89   C

The Act imposes obligations on the Data Controller (an individual or an organisation who has information about the individual), and the rights of the Data Subject (individual about whom the information is held).

90   A

The other three rights are the right of subject access (to be given a description of the personal data); to prevent processing likely to cause damage or distress, and the right to request that the Commissioner assesses whether any contravention of the Act has occurred.

91   FALSE

There are many Health and Safety hazards in any workplace, such as fire, faulty electrical equipment or even unsound shelving units.

92   FALSE

The employee is responsible for his or her own health and safety. The employer has a duty to provide a safe working environment, etc.

MACROECONOMIC FACTORS

93   B

This is sometimes referred to as demand-deficient, persistent or Keynesian unemployment. Keynesian economists refer to this as a deflationary gap and would seek to remove it by boosting demand. Monetarists would seek to reduce cyclical unemployment by appropriate supply side measures as they would argue that cyclical unemployment does not really exist.

94   A

By increasing their exchange rate (so that it is more expensive relative to other currencies), the country with the trade surplus will make their exports more expensive. This will reduce the attractiveness of their exports and should result in a lower trade surplus.

95   C

Microeconomics is the study of small firms and individual consumers and industries. Macroeconomics is the study of the aggregate economic behaviour of nations.

96   D

Growth is concerned with increasing productive capacity; inflation refers to ensuring that general price levels do not increase; unemployment refers to ensuring that everyone who wants a job has one; balance of payments refers to managing our trade with other countries.

97   D

Expectations are often self-fulfilling as people adjust their behaviour based on the predictions made, such as the belief that house prices will continue to grow will cause people to buy a house to make a quick gain, which in its turn inflates the prices of houses.

98   B

Having a budget deficit means that the government is putting money in the economy, for example by employing more people, who will use their earning to buy goods produced in the country, thus giving jobs to even more people. C and D are a part of the monetary policy.

99   FALSE

Keynes was an advocate of demand side policies.

100   D

A recession starts when demand begins to fall and leads to reduced purchases of raw materials and increased unemployment; this in turn leads to reduced household incomes and a further fall in demand, which can result in a slump.

101   A

In extreme cases of inflation the function of money may break down, leading to civil unrest and even war.

102   B

The Monetary Policy Committee of the Bank of England has been responsible for setting interest rates since 1997. They set rates with a view to meeting the Government's inflation target.

103   B

The country is exporting too much, which means that factors of production could be fully utilised, therefore the costs of an additional unit of output will be higher than the costs of previous units, thus prices will be raised causing inflation.

104 B

In the UK, VAT (same rate for everyone) and road taxes (same amount for everyone) are examples of regressive taxes.

105 C

Growth should result in more goods demanded and produced, people earning more and more jobs.

106 D

'Demerit' goods are such things as illegal drugs. A, B and C are examples of the positive aspects of growth. A = real growth. B = the benefits of growth are being evenly distributed. C = the population, on average, is better off.

107 A

Keynes argued that it was the government's role to move the economy to a better equilibrium, i.e. one closer to full employment. This involved the government borrowing money and injecting it into the economy to stimulate economic growth – or slowing down the economy by increasing levels of taxation.

108 TRUE

Supply side economics focus on improving the supply of factors of production in an economy.

109 D

The four factors generate income as follows: Labour = Wages; Land = Rents; Capital = Interest; Entrepreneurship = Profits.

110 B

Imports weaken the currency and increase the cost of imports; monetary inflation arises from an over expansion of the money supply; expectations built into wage negotiations and pricing decisions tend to increase the rate of inflation.

SOCIAL AND TECHNOLOGICAL FACTORS

111 C

To maximise the economic growth, the government tries to make sure that employment levels are high.

112 C

Outsourcing means that some of the processes previously undertaken by the company itself are now being transferred to an external supplier.

113 TRUE

The population of the UK grew by 7.7% between 1971 and 2006. Over the same period the number of dwellings grew by 35%.

114 B

Such older mothers are more demanding of the baby products they buy.

115 D

Carbon footprint refers to the volume of carbon emissions produced by the company. The goal of social responsibility is to be conscious of the impact operations have on the environment and the planet. It is possible for the firm's products to be boycotted if customers believe that it acts in a socially irresponsible way.

116 C

Delayering refers to the reduction in the number of levels of management, making organisational structure flatter. Managers can use technology to help keep in touch with staff, thus freeing more time for more urgent tasks. Option D is not directly relevant to organisational structure.

COMPETITIVE FACTORS

117 C

Threat of substitutes refers to people's tendency to replace one product with another.

118 D

The assessment will be in three steps, analysing how the firm can achieve a competitive advantage, the main competitive forces in the industry and how parts of the firm contribute to its competitiveness.

119 B

The first choice is between lower costs and differentiation and the second is the scope of the area in which the company wishes to obtain competitive advantage.

120 TRUE

Focus strategy means that all of a company's activities are directed towards serving a niche market.

121 D

Outbound logistics includes packaging and delivery.

122 D

Looking at an individual firm, its ability to earn higher profit margins will be determined by whether or not it can manage the five forces more effectively than competitors.

123   B

The approach involves breaking the firm down into five 'primary' and four 'support' activities and then looking at each to see if they give a cost advantage or quality advantage.

STAKEHOLDERS

124   A

Internal includes employees and managers/directors; connected includes shareholders, customers, suppliers, and finance providers. The third stakeholder group is external which includes the community at large, government and trade unions.

125   C

When the company is not able to generate profit, it is unlikely to pay staff wages or even survive.

126   TRUE

Customers have an interest in higher levels of product and service quality and, in the short term at least, satisfying this interest is likely to reduce the profits and dividends available to shareholders.

127   C

Shareholders have a high level of power, but a low level of interest.

128   FALSE

This approach is referred to as Keep Informed, whereas minimal effort implies that stakeholders will accept what they are told.

COMMITTEES IN THE BUSINESS ORGANISATION

129   A

Ad-hoc stands for 'for the purpose' and the committee is likely to be disbanded as soon as the issue for which it was created is resolved.

130   D

Part of the Chairman's role is to maintain order, whereas A, B and C are a part of the role of Secretary.

131   B

Other duties of the committee secretary include preparing the location; assisting the chair; acting on and communicating decisions.

132 D

More work can be undertaken than individuals working alone; delegation of authority could be to a sub-committee.

133 FALSE

The remuneration committee is usually focused on Director's remuneration package.

134 C

These are three important elements of a successful committee. A, B and D also list important elements – save for the third item in each case.

135 TRUE

Other purposes are to promote the smooth running of the committee; to enable both sides in an argument to state their case and to ensure a proper record of all the proceedings is kept.

BUSINESS ETHICS AND BEHAVIOUR

136 B

An integrity based approach encourages the company to do the right things and emphasises managerial responsibility for ethical behaviour as a well as a concern for the law.

137 B

The remaining two ethical principles are integrity and objectivity.

138 TRUE

Those failing to observe the standards expected of them may be called before the ACCA's Disciplinary Committee and required to explain their conduct.

139 B

Ethics is concerned with good/bad and with what you should/ought to do. The other statements are factual statements with no ethical content.

140 TRUE

The IFAC code (which is the basis of the ACCA code) states in its introduction that 'a professional accountant's responsibility is not exclusively to satisfy the needs of an individual client or employer.'

141 D

The professional accountant, therefore, has a duty to act in the public interest as well as in the interests of his employer and the shareholders.

142   A

Delaying payments to suppliers is an inappropriate business practice. In situations B and C it is rectifying the results of its previous doubtful actions. Option D is an example of a company's ethical aspirations.

143   TRUE

Breaches of the code can result in members being admonished, fined, suspended or excluded from membership.

For example, in 2004 an ACCA member was excluded from membership having been convicted of three counts of false accounting.

GOVERNANCE AND SOCIAL RESPONSIBILITY

144   B

The modern view is that a coherent Corporate Social Responsibility strategy can offer business benefits.

This is particularly true of the oil industry where major UK and US companies have attracted very substantial criticism as a result of an apparent failure to adequately protect the environment from oil spills.

145   D

Reasons for the separation of ownership and control include the suggestion that specialist management can run the business better than those who own the business.

146   D

Directors, who are placed in control of resources that they do not own and are effectively agents of the shareholders, should be working in the best interests of the shareholders. However, they may be tempted to act in their own interests, for example by voting themselves huge salaries. The background to the agency problem is the separation of ownership and control – in many large companies the people who own the company (the shareholders) are not the same people as those who control the company (the board of directors).

147   B

As this will serve as a financial motivator and will align directors' interests with organisational ones.

148   D

Other key issues are membership of the board of directors (both executive and non-executive) and the role of the board of directors. (Purely to make money for the shareholders or are there wider responsibilities?)

149   B

The stakeholders are all those influenced by, or those who can influence, the company's decisions and actions.

150 B

Sustainable development focuses on the future, making sure that our actions today do not jeopardise the future of the planet.

151 A

Many customers are choosing to buy Fairtrade products and shareholders are investing in environmentally-friendly companies as people are becoming more aware of the impact their actions have on the environment and society as a whole.

152 C

Balance scorecard considers four perspectives: Financial, Innovation and Learning, Customer and Internal business ones. The approach highlights the importance of success as being measured against the above set of criteria rather than purely through financial results.

153 D

Owning the shares creates a direct link between a company's performance and the NED's wealth, thus rendering him/her non-independent.

154 FALSE

Most codes on Corporate Governance state that no director should be involved in deciding the level of their own remuneration.

155 D

A board can also give them work to do that ensures that they go nowhere near areas where the directors know there are mistakes or fraud.

156 A

An audit committee should, amongst other things, review accounting policies and financial statements as a whole to ensure that they are appropriate and balanced.

157 B

Companies are required by law to send a copy (or a summarised version) to each shareholder. Most companies will post a copy on their web site or will provide a paper-based copy free of charge to any member of the public who requests one.

LAW AND REGULATION GOVERNING ACCOUNTING

158 D

Companies house deals with incorporation and dissolution on companies, as it examines and stores companies' information as per Companies Act requirements.

159 TRUE

The Companies Act leaves a scope of interpretation of 'true and fair'.

160   D

In order to prepare true and fair financial statements companies have to maintain 'proper accounting records' which are sufficient to show and explain the transactions.

The content of the records is not defined, but a record of transactions, assets and liabilities would be required as a minimum.

161   A

It is a criminal offence which could lead to prosecution.

The collapse of Enron (which had grown rapidly to become America's seventh largest company) in 2001 is probably the best known recent example of failure to maintain proper accounting records. It was found that senior staff at Enron had lied about its profits and a number of senior executives were convicted and imprisoned. The Enron scandal contributed to the Sarbanes Oxley Act of 2002 which imposed much more demanding reporting requirements upon US companies.

162   D

Some errors in financial statements are inevitable so they will never be entirely accurate. Similarly an unqualified audit report does not mean that there has been no fraud – if a fraud is not material then it will not cause a material misstatement.

163   C

The IASB's aims are to develop a single set of high quality, understandable and enforceable global accounting standards and to co-operate with national accounting standard-setters to achieve convergence in accounting standards around the world.

164   D

Because the matters covered are quite narrowly defined, an interpretation can be issued relatively quickly.

A, B and C describe, respectively, the roles of the IASB (International Accounting Standards Board), the IASCF (International Accounting Standards Committee Foundation) and the SAC (Standards Advisory Council).

THE ACCOUNTING PROFESSION

165   TRUE

Forecasting is often made difficult by the unpredictability of the environment in which the company operates, that is why both quantitative and qualitative information must be considered before arriving to a definitive conclusion.

166   D

Limited liability companies are the dominant economic force in the business world. Quoted companies are normally limited liability companies. There are large numbers of sole traders and partnerships but they are far less significant in economic terms.

167 C

As managers have all the information about the company and then produce the financial statement, this statement needs to be independently verified to make sure all the information is presented fairly.

168 FALSE

References to accounting appearin the Bible and the Koran. Luca Pacioli was the first person to print the book summarising the idea of double-entry bookkeeping.

169 D

Accounting function is responsible for maintaining adequate records so as to enable management to make decisions.

ACCOUNTING AND FINANCE FUNCTIONS

170 C

The treasurer would also be responsible for debt strategy, currency management, banking forecasting and risk management.

171 B

Strategic planning is concerned with long-term problems external to the current business, in particular with deciding which products or services to produce for which markets.

172 D

Companies must send a copy of their financial statements to each shareholder each year.

173 A

Small companies do not have to be audited. As the company is owner-managed the agency problem will not be relevant.

174 C

The books of prime entry include sales, payables ledger, cash and petty cash books and appropriate journals.

175 D

Break even analysis focuses on the time period after which the project starts to generate profit. The shorter the period, the less risk the project involves.

176 FALSE

This is tax evasion as the company is illegally reducing its tax liability.

177 D

Tax avoidance is used to describe schemes which, whilst they are legal, are designed to defeat the intentions of the law makers. Thus, once a tax avoidance scheme becomes public knowledge, the law makers will usually step in to change the law to stop the scheme from working.

178 C

A, B and D are not true. They describe advantages of using the issue of share capital to finance investment.

179 A

Working capital is the capital available for conducting the day-to-day operations of an organisation.

FINANCIAL SYSTEMS AND PROCEDURES

180 TRUE

Businesses that wish to fraudulently overstate or understate their profits (to reduce their tax bill) can be tempted to understate or overstate either the physical quantities of inventory held or the values placed upon them.

181 B

Staff will be more careful when dealing with fragile items. A is not a long-term solution, whereas C and D are impractical.

182 D

Credit notes are issued to adjust incorrect invoices; this could be due to goods being returned or the original invoice being of a wrong value.

183 FALSE

Transactions which do not follow the procedure, which could be error or fraud, can be identified more easily.

184 A

Each specific income/expense type is given a unique code number and invoices relating to that income/expense type are coded with that number.

185 D

Customer identity and ability to pay should be verified prior to a sale being processed. A, B, and C are good control measures, but are not directly relevant to prompt payment.

186 B

BACS is an automated bank transfer when the money is sent directly to an employee's bank account, which makes the transaction easy to trace and more secure.

187 C

A cheque requisition should be prepared for each payment. The cheque, the cheque requisition and the invoices to be paid should be submitted to a senior manager for approval and to have the cheque signed. Two signatories are often required for cheques above a certain amount. All cheques should be approved, not just large ones.

188 TRUE

The usual procedure is for the individual responsible for the petty cash to present the receipts and vouchers in order to obtain replenishment.

189 D

The purposes of organisational control are to safeguard company assets, ensure efficiency and prevent fraud and errors.

190 FALSE

Two people should open the post and list the contents.

191 D

Ghost employees are used to defraud the company via the company payroll.

192 C

Errors in manual systems can be corrected via use of whitening fluid, etc.

In fact, automated systems have fewer errors, more security (passwords) and are easier to audit than manual systems.

THE RELATIONSHIP OF ACCOUNTING WITH OTHER BUSINESS FUNCTIONS

193 D

The accounting department can advise on the maximum price that should be paid to maintain margins.

194 TRUE

A steering committee normally deals with projects, so a project on implementing a new accounting system would need both IT and accounting representatives to come together to discuss the finer details of the process.

195 B

This is a philosophy of business that permeates all areas, focusing attention on the customer.

A = a sales orientation. D = a product orientation.

196 D

There are four basic elements of the marketing mix: Product / Place / Promotion / Price which are known as the '4Ps'.

197 C

Product definition = defining exactly what the product should be. Product positioning = how does our product compare with the offerings of our competitors?

198 A

A low price is set to gain market share, e.g. new magazines often have special reduced prices for the first two or three months.

199 C

The first product is cheap to attract customers but the second is expensive, e.g. printers and printer cartridges.

200 TRUE

Selling direct means that the manufacturer sells directly to the ultimate consumer without using any middlemen, e.g. accountancy firms deal directly with their clients. Selling indirect means using a channel strategy that could comprise a mixture of retailers, distributors, wholesalers and shipping agents.

201 D

Analysis will include analysis of brand strength, product quality, competition, etc. Choice will include decisions regarding which products to sell and segmenting potential markets.Implementation will include setting budgets, targets for sales revenue, etc.

202 D

Desk research makes use of information which already exists; field research involves asking people for their views on different products and test marketing involves a test marketing campaign in a typical area which possesses the required promotional facilities.

203 FALSE

Segmentation is done first, which means the market is divided into homogenous customer groups. Then, targeting is then used to decide which group of customers to focus on.

INTERNAL AND EXTERNAL AUDIT

204 B

The internal audit also makes recommendations for the achievement of company objectives.

C is the role of the external auditors.

205 TRUE

Directors need reassurance on financial matters other than the financial statements and this reassurance can be provided by the internal auditors.

206 A

Where there is an internal audit function, the board should annually review its scope of work, authority and resources.

207 B

They are employed by the management of the company and yet are expected to give an objective opinion on matters for which management are responsible.

208 D

The audit committee would act as an interface between the directors and internal auditors to reduce the problem of independence.

209 B

The internal auditors may be unwilling to disclose the existence of fraud because the repercussions could, at worst, involve the collapse of the company and the resulting loss of their jobs. Such circumstances surrounding the loss of their jobs may also make it difficult for them to secure another job.

210 FALSE

Substantive testing is aimed at substantiating and verifying the figures and balances in the financial statement.

211 FALSE

There is currently no legal requirement in the UK to appoint internal auditors.

212 TRUE

Guidance for an internal audit is limited to fundamental principles and a small quantity of standards and these factors are largely responsible for the greater flexibility in how the work is done.

213 FALSE

There is no legal requirement for an internal auditor to possess an accounting qualification, though it is highly desirable.

INTERNAL FINANCIAL CONTROL

214 A

Control environment refers to the overall attitude of managers to the importance of internal controls.

215 C

The principal reason why internal controls interest the external auditor is that reliance on internal controls will reduce the amount of substantive testing required of transactions and the resultant balances in the ledger accounts.

216 B

As it would be best that the manager approves a transaction before the money is given back to the customer.

217 FALSE

The passwords need to be individual so as to leave the activity trail so all transactions could be traced to the person who has recorded them.

218 B

There should be a division of responsibilities for authorising or initiating a transaction, the physical custody and control of assets involved, and recording the transaction.

219 B

There are two other objectives with regard to effectiveness and efficiency of operations and compliance with applicable laws and regulations.

220 C

Each individual's work is subject to an independent check by another person in the course of that other person's duties.

221 B

It is particularly important that stringent controls exist where there are associated legal requirements.

222 A

The presence of a supervisor may deter people from committing fraud, such as taking money out of the till. B and C are an example of detective controls, D is an example of a corrective control.

223 TRUE

The auditor will be interested not just in whether there are sufficient controls, but in examples of over-control and inefficiencies.

224 A

Business risk is conventionally split between internal and external factors. Once the risks have been identified, management must investigate their significance, the likelihood of their occurrence and how they should be managed.

225 D

Physical controls also include access controls, key-locked cabinets, CCTV and so on.

226 C

The 1999 Turnbull report emphasises that 'The board of directors is responsible for the company's system of internal controls'.

FRAUD

227 FALSE

The third prerequisite is dishonesty. An honest employee is unlikely to commit fraud even if given the opportunity and motive.

228 B

The fraudster hopes that no one will notice or bother to investigate the small differences individually, although in aggregate they can total a worthwhile sum.

229 D

This fraud is covered up by misposting future receipts to the accounts which earlier had not been credited.

This fraud is often uncovered when the perpetrator takes a holiday and is unable to make the necessary mispostings to cover his tracks.

230 B

These transactions are often reversed out after the year end.

Typically, sales made just before the year end are the subject of inflated invoices which are corrected by the issue of credit notes in the new year.

231 D

An example is a two-year lease of a building. Under current accounting practices you do not have to show the asset or the related obligation to pay the rental amounts on the balance sheet. However, you have the use of the asset and a contractual obligation to pay the rentals.

232 FALSE

In practice many organisations find that fraud is impossible eradicate. With regards to error, as it is unintentional, it will be hard to prevent such mistakes from taking place.

233 FALSE

There is an implied duty within an employment contract so as to encourage staff to be honest and report any actual or suspected fraud.

234 FALSE

The auditors' primary concern is to establish whether the accounts give a true and fair view. Only if the incident of fraud was material in value, and it is not properly reflected in the financial statement, would the auditors need to qualify the financial statement.

235 C

People living beyond their means are often driven to make up the shortfall of money necessary to support such a luxury lifestyle by committing fraud.

RECRUITMENT AND SELECTION, MANAGING DIVERSITY AND EQUAL OPPORTUNITY

236 D

The job advertisement should be positive and honest about the organisation.

The temptation is to overstate the attractions of the job in order to boost the number of applicants.

237 D

Individuals with specific skills are likely to be in receipt of trade, technical or professional journals (e.g. Accountancy Age) and accustomed to using those journals to find a job.

A disadvantage of such journals is that they can have long closing dates and may contain many similar advertisements.

238 B

The personal specification is focused on the attributes a candidate needs to posses in order to fulfil the job requirements. The job description is focused on duties and responsibilities of the post, whereas job evaluation considers the worth of the job to the company and therefore how much the jobholder is to be paid.

239 FALSE

Recruitment consultants are usually involved in the early stages of the recruitment and selection process, e.g. advising on job descriptions, designing job advertisements, screening applications and assisting with short-listing of candidates for interview. They frequently conduct the first round of interviews.

Consultants are not normally involved in deciding which of the short-listed candidates should get the job.

240 A

Economic uncertainty tends to encourage employees to remain in their present jobs, particularly if they have a family to support.

241 D

The attributes of the ideal candidate would be set out in the Person Specification.

242 C

There is often little incentive for the past employer to give extensive references, but the company has a duty to provide a response which needs to be factual.

243 TRUE

The two other key elements of an interview are to find the best person for the job and to ensure that the candidate understands what the job is and what the career prospects are. The interviewing process also impacts on the company's image.

244 D

Diversity is perceived to enrich an organisation's human capital.

245 B

Some organisations set themselves goals on the representation of certain groups to address the problem of under-representation.

246 B

This legislation typically also outlines the different forms of discrimination being direct, indirect, victimisation and harassment.

247 C

'Halo' effect related to the interviewer making up his/hers mind about the candidate based on secondary factors such as manner and personality rather than considering the person's ability to do the job.

248 D

Assessment centre allows a company to test candidates' capability through engaging in role plays, having team-based exercises and doing presentations amongst other things.

249 C

As part of the engagement process, the preferred candidate is sent a job offer letter, employment contract and a staff handbook which he/she needs to sign and return.

250 D

To make a new recruit becomes effective quickly, he/she needs to be properly introduced into the company by getting to know the colleagues, having a company's policies explained and having a tour of the facilities.

REVIEW AND APPRAISAL OF INDIVIDUAL PERFORMANCE

251 C

Appraisal is based on assessing an employee's past performance, therefore the results produced should be given a thorough consideration.

252 B

The task-centred method relates to what the subordinate is doing and how they do it.

Review and comparison involves both review of results achieved and comparison with agreed statements of required results.

Management by objectives involves a review of results achieved against certain objectives agreed with the manager involved.

253 FALSE

A self-appraisal form gives a chance to a member of staff to formulate his/her opinion on his/her own performance and also gives the manager a valuable insight into what issues might need to be addressed during the appraisal interview.

254 D

Effective appraisal is also grounded in the belief that:

- the process of isolating and rewarding good performance is likely to encourage the employee to repeat it

- agreement on challenging and achievable targets for performance motivates employees by clarifying goals and setting the value of incentives offered.

255 TRUE

Discharge – as a result of an employee's unsuitability, disciplinary action or redundancy. Unavoidable – because of marriage, moving house, illness or death.　　　　　Avoidable – due to pay, working conditions, relationships with work colleagues.

256 FALSE

One should divide by the **average** number in the workforce.

257 B

Appraisals often discuss issues such as problems encountered by the employee during the period, or even pay rises. Therefore having other people around may distract the parties from having a frank and open discussion.

258 TRUE

Succession planning refers to preparing the next generation of managers. Appraisal helps to identify the strengths and weaknesses of an individual employee and helps to map the path to taking on a more senior role.

TRAINING DEVELOPMENT AND LEARNING

259 B

Evening classes or day release would be suitable for the significant amount of studying that the trainee accountant will need to undertake whilst the till operator needs the 'hands on' experience that is provided by on-the-job training.

260 C

Learning includes the acquisition of a new skill, new knowledge, a modified attitude or a combination of all three.

261 A

This is known as the learning curve. The shape of the learning curve depends on the type of work or task and the individual.

262 FALSE

A learner can start at any stage, but the whole cycle needs to be completed for the knowledge to be fully acquired.

263 TRUE

Learning in the workplace fosters increased competence and flexibility in times of constant change and there is growing evidence that a learning culture can increase the productivity and competitiveness of organisations.

264 FALSE

There is increasing recognition that the pace of change is accelerating and that the most successful companies will be those with workforces that have the opportunity to keep abreast of the changes and are encouraged to develop their knowledge and skills through CPD programmes.

265 A

An activist is a learner that needs a constant inflow of new ideas, he/she is constantly searching for new challenges and is likely to be exposed to such experiences when interacting with a group.

266 B

According to Kolb, people who have a clear learning style preference, for whatever reason, will tend to learn more effectively if learning is geared to their preference.

267 FALSE

A training gap refers to any **shortfall** of knowledge, understanding, skill or attitudes, rather than a surplus.

268 A

Management development looks at an individual's competencies to ensure he/she has sufficient exposure to various organisational functions to be prepared for an increase in responsibility.

269 A

It is equally important that management should seek to transform the continuous learning and acquisition of new knowledge and skills into actual behaviour, products and processes within the organisation.

270 FALSE

Work shadowing often involves learning by observation and repetition. A mentor is a senior and more experienced member of staff who helps the trainee to develop in both personal and career terms by giving guidance and support.

271 FALSE

Hamblin's fifth level of evaluation seeks to asses the ultimate value of the training in areas such as profitability, survival and growth of the organisation as a whole.

IMPROVING PERSONAL EFFECTIVENESS AT WORK

272 TRUE

Development has no immediate practical application but over time it enables a person to deal with wider problems.

273 B

PDP is an action plan aimed to allow the individual to develop; therefore we first need to consider the personal aspirations and objectives.

274 D

Stage 1 = personal SWOT (strengths, weaknesses, opportunities, threats);

Stage 2 = Set goals, involving identifying particular weaknesses;

Stage 3 = Draw up an action plan based on addressing the identified weaknesses.

275 B

Other important time management techniques are producing an activity log/spending time planning and organising/prioritising/costing your time.

276 C

Opportunity cost calculation could also involve costing personal time to see what would be the most value-adding way to prioritise work.

277 FALSE

Counselling is about helping people to help themselves; it helps people to address their worries and anxieties created by relationships, uncertainty or problems within the individual him/herself.

278 D

Exchange of knowledge that is unique to a business, industry, profession or organisation. The third core objective is the measurable beneficial outcomes for the individual parties involved and for the larger organisation.

279 FALSE

Counselling is non-directive; the individual is to decide him/herself what is to be achieved and the best ways to do so.

280 TRUE

First generation followers limit their time management efforts to keeping lists and notes. Fourth generation people understand the difference between urgency and importance.

281 D

Being effective means getting the result that you want.

There are a variety of planning aids (e.g. electronic personal organisers and hand-held computerised diaries) to support and improve personal productivity.

EFFECTIVE COMMUNICATION AND INTERPERSONAL SKILLS

282 FALSE

A grapevine network connects people who have a common interest and usually circulates rumours and gossip.

283 A

Communication is the interchange of information, ideas, facts and emotions by two or more people.

284 FALSE

Research has established that only 10% of the message is communicated through words, the other 90% is transmitted through non-verbal communication.

285 TRUE

Most companies can produce such examples of instructions, control reports, etc which are distributed on the basis of seniority or status.

286 D

Failure to remove communication barriers can have very serious consequences for the organisation. General rules to ensure communication is effective include avoiding communication overload, ensuring the right information gets to the right person at the right time, and agreeing and confirming priorities and deadlines for receipt of information.

287 FALSE

Barriers to communication also include anything that stops information from being understood by its recipients or being acted upon in the way intended.

Barriers to communication can be caused by many things, e.g. 'noise' (message confused by extraneous matters); difference in education levels; overload (too much information); distortion of information by the receiver; use of technical or professional language.

288 B

Lateral is another name for horizontal communication, within a committee people from different functions come together to present their view on an issue.

289 C

The communication process starts with the sender formulating a message, then it is encoded using an appropriate format, transmitted through a medium, received, decoded and a response is given to the sender.

290 A

In the centralised networks (chain, wheel and 'Y'), group members have to go through a person located in the central position in the network in order to communicate with others. In the decentralised networks (circle and all-channels), information can flow freely between members without having to go through a central person.

291 TRUE

Information overload is one of the barriers to communication; it makes it difficult to prioritise.

292 TRUE

The level of satisfaction for individuals is fairly high in the all-channel andmixed in the wheel, with the central figures usually expressing greater satisfaction and the rest feeling isolated.

293 C

The wheel was shown to be the quickest way to reach a conclusion.

294 D

Under time pressure the all-channels system either restructures (to form a wheel) or disintegrates.

295 B

The all-channel is the most likely process to reach the best decision.

Section 3

PILOT PAPER QUESTIONS

1   Span of control is concerned with the number of levels of management in an organisation.

Is this statement true or false?

A   True

B   False

(1 mark)

2   Which of the following is the main function of marketing?

A   To maximise sales volume

B   To identify and anticipate customer needs

C   To persuade potential consumers to convert latent demand into expenditure

D   To identify suitable outlets for goods and services supplied

(2 marks)

3   Which one of the following has become an established best practice in corporate governance in recent years?

A   An increasingly prominent role for non-executive directors

B   An increase in the powers of external auditors

C   Greater accountability for directors who are in breach of their fiduciary duties

D   A requirement for all companies to establish an internal audit function

(2 marks)

4   According to Charles Handy's four cultural stereotypes, which of the following organisations would adopt a task culture?

A   The cost accounting department of a large steel producing company

B   The consulting division of a 'big four' accountancy firm

C   A civil service department

D   A small clothes and design fashion house

(2 marks)

5 **At what stage of the planning process should a company carry out a situation analysis?**

    A   When converting strategic objectives into tactical plans

    B   When formulating a mission statement

    C   When validating the effectiveness of plans against outcomes

    D   When formulating strategic objectives

    (2 marks)

6 **Which one of the following is a potential advantage of decentralisation?**

    A   Greater control by senior management

    B   Risk reduction in relation to operational decision making

    C   More accountability at lower levels

    D   Consistency of decision making across the organisation

    (2 marks)

7 **Which one of the following is an example of a internal stakeholder?**

    A   A shareholder

    B   An non-executive director

    C   A manager

    D   A supplier

    (2 marks)

8 **According to Mendelow, companies must pay most attention to the needs of which group of stakeholders?**

    A   Those with little power and little interest in the company

    B   Those with a high level of power, but little interest in the company

    C   Those with little power, but a high level of interest in the company

    D   Those with a high level of power and a high level of interest in the company

    (2 marks)

9 **What is the responsibility of a Public Oversight Board?**

    A   The establishment of detailed rules on internal audit procedures

    B   The commissioning of financial reporting standards

    C   The creation of legislation relating to accounting standards

    D   The monitoring and enforcement of legal and compliance standards

    (2 marks)

10   The ageing population trend in many European countries is caused by a increasing birth rate and an increasing mortality rate.

Is this statement true or false?

A   True

B   False

(1 mark)

11   Which one of the following is consistent with a government's policy objective to expand the level of economic activity?

A   An increase in taxation

B   An increase in interest rates

C   An increase in personal savings

D   An increase in public expenditure

(2 marks)

12   Which of the following is the name given to unemployment arising from labour in the market place being of the wrong type or available in the wrong place?

A   Structural unemployment

B   Cyclical unemployment

C   Frictional unemployment

D   Marginal unemployment

(2 marks)

13   When an organisation carries out an environmental scan, it analyses which of the following?

A   Strengths, weaknesses, opportunities and threats

B   Political, economic, social and technological factors

C   Strategic options and choice

D   Inbound and outbound logistics

(2 marks)

14   Which of the following is data protection legislation primarily designed to protect?

A   All private individuals and corporate entities on whom only regulated data is held

B   All private individuals on whom only regulated data is held

C   All private individuals on whom any data is held

D   All private individuals and corporate entities on whom any data is held

(2 marks)

15 **Which of the following types of new legislation would provide greater employment opportunities in large companies?**

   A   New laws on health and safety

   B   New laws to prevent discrimination in the workplace

   C   New laws making it more difficult to dismiss employees unfairly

   D   New laws on higher compensation for employer breaches of employment contracts

   (2 marks)

16 **The total level of demand in the economy is made up of consumption, _____, government expenditure and net gains from international trade.**

   Which of the following correctly completes the sentence above?

   A   Savings

   B   Taxation

   C   Investment

   (1 mark)

17 **Which set of environmental factors does a lobby group intend to directly influence?**

   A   Political

   B   Technological

   C   Demographic

   D   Economic

   (2 marks)

18 **The use of advanced technology solutions in order to maximise the productivity and effectiveness of call centre operations is an application of the principles established by which school of management thought?**

   A   Human relations

   B   Empirical

   C   Scientific

   D   Administrative

   (2 marks)

19 **The original role of the accounting function was which one of the following?**

   A   Providing management information

   B   Recording financial information

   C   Maintaining financial control

   D   Managing funds efficiently

   (2 marks)

20 Tax avoidance is a legal activity whilst tax evasion is an illegal activity.

Is this statement true or false?

A   True

B   False

(1 mark)

21 The system used by a company to record sales and purchases is an example of which of the following?

A   A transaction processing system

B   A management information system

C   An office automation system

D   A decision support system

(2 marks)

22 The implementation of a budgetary control system in a large organisation would be the responsibility of the internal auditor.

Is this statement true or false?

A   True

B   False

(1 mark)

23 Which type of organisation would have the retail prices it charges to personal consumers subject to close scrutiny by a regulator?

A   A multinational corporation

B   A multi-divisional conglomerate

C   A national utilities company

D   A financial services provider

(2 marks)

24 The central bank has announced a 2% increase in interest rates.

This decision has the most impact on which department of a large company?

A   Marketing

B   Treasury

C   Financial accounting

D   Production

(2 marks)

25 The major purpose of the International Accounting Standards Board (IASB) is to ensure consistency in _____.

Which two words complete this sentence?

A   Financial control

B   Corporate reporting

C   External auditing

(1 mark)

26 X Co has a financial accountant and a management accountant.

Which group of activities would fall within the responsibility of the financial accountant?

A   Payroll, purchase ledger, sales invoicing

B   Inventory valuation, budgetary control and variance analysis

C   Fraud avoidance, segregation of duties, internal review and control

D   Funds management, risk assessment, project and investment appraisal

(2 marks)

27 In an economic environment of high price inflation, those who owe money will gain and those who are owed money will lose.

Is this statement true or false?

A   True

B   False

(1 mark)

28 To whom is the internal auditor primarily accountable?

A   The directors of the company

B   The company as a separate entity

C   The shareholders of the company

D   The employees of the company

(2 marks)

29 Which one of the following is a DISADVANTAGE of a computerised accounting system over a manual accounting system?

A   A computerised system is more time consuming to operate

B   The operating costs of a computerised system are higher

C   The computerised system is more costly to implement

D   A computerised system is more error prone

(2 marks)

30 The identification, evaluation, testing and reporting on internal controls is a feature of which of the following?

    A   Operational audit

    B   Transactions audit

    C   Social responsibility audit

    D   Systems audit

(2 marks)

31 What is the primary responsibility of the external auditor?

    A   To verify all the financial transactions and supporting documentation of the client

    B   To ensure that the client's financial statements are reasonably accurate and free from bias

    C   To report all financial irregularities to the shareholders of the client

    D   To ensure that all the client's financial statements are prepared and submitted to the relevant authorities on time

(2 marks)

32 Which of the following are substantive tests used for, in the context of external audit of financial accounts?

    A   To establish whether a figure is correct

    B   To investigate why a figure is incorrect

    C   To investigate whether a figure should be included

    D   To establish why a figure is excluded

(2 marks)

33 In the context of fraud, 'teeming and lading' is most likely to occur in which area of operation?

    A   Sales

    B   Quality control

    C   Advertising and promotion

    D   Despatch

(2 marks)

34 In order to establish an effective internal control system that will minimise the prospect of fraud, which one of the following should be considered first?

    A   Recruitment policy and checks on new personnel

    B   Identification of areas of potential risk

    C   Devising of appropriate sanctions for inappropriate behaviour

    D   Segregation of duties in critical areas

(2 marks)

35 The leadership style that least acknowledges the contribution that subordinates have to make is _____.

Which word correctly completes this sentence?

A   Authoritarian

B   Autocratic

C   Assertive

(1 mark)

36 The Blake and Mouton managerial grid examines the relationship between 'concern for production' and which of the following?

A   concern for people

B   concern for sales

C   concern for quality

D   concern for service

(2 marks)

37 Jackie leads an established team of six workers. In the last month, two have left to pursue alternative jobs and one has commenced maternity leave. Three new staff members have joined Jackie's team.

Which one of Tuckman's group stages will now occur?

A   Norming

B   Forming

C   Performing

D   Storming

(2 marks)

38 Richard is a valuable member of his team. He is enthusiastic and curious, highly communicative and has a capacity for contacting people and exploring anything new.

Which of Belbin's team roles does Richard fulfil?

A   Monitor-evaluator

B   Plant

C   Resource-investigator

D   Company worker

(2 marks)

39 Which one of the following statements is correct in relation to monetary rewards in accordance with Herzberg's Two-Factor theory?

A   Pay increases are a powerful long-term motivator

B   Inadequate monetary rewards are a powerful dissatisfier

C   Monetary rewards are more important than non-monetary rewards

D   Pay can never be used as a motivator

(2 marks)

40 Which one of the following is a characteristic of a team as opposed to a group?

A   Members agree with other members

B   Members negotiate personal roles and positions

C   Members arrive at decisions by consensus

D   Members work in cooperation

(2 marks)

41 According to Victor Vroom: Force (or motivation) = _____ x expectancy

Which of the following words completes Vroom's equation?

A   Needs

B   Valence

C   Opportunity

(1 mark)

42 According to Handy's 'shamrock' organisation model, which one of the following is becoming progressively less important in contemporary organisations?

A   The permanent, full-time work force

B   The part-time temporary work force

C   The role of independent sub-contractors

D   The role of technical support functions

(2 marks)

43 Which pattern of communication is the quickest way to send a message?

A   The circle

B   The chain

C   The Y

D   The wheel

(2 marks)

44 **Poor quality lateral communication will result in which of the following?**

    A   Lack of direction

    B   Lack of coordination

    C   Lack of delegation

    D   Lack of control

(2 marks)

45 **Role playing exercises using video recording and playback would be most effective for which type of training?**

    A   Development of selling skills

    B   Regulation and compliance

    C   Dissemination of technical knowledge

    D   Introduction of new processes or procedures

(2 marks)

46 **In the context of marketing, the 'four P's' are price, place, promotion and _____ .**

Which word correctly completes this sentence?

    A   Processes

    B   Production

    C   Product

(1 mark)

47 **In relation to employee selection, which type of testing is most appropriate for assessing the depth of knowledge of a candidate and the candidate's ability to apply that knowledge?**

    A   Intelligence testing

    B   Personality testing

    C   Competence testing

    D   Psychometric testing

(2 marks)

48 **A company has advertised for staff who must be at least 1.88 metres tall and have been in continuous full-time employment for at least five years.**

Which of the following is the legal term for this unlawful practice?

    A   Direct discrimination

    B   Indirect discrimination

    C   Victimisation

    D   Implied discrimination

(2 marks)

49   Which one of the following is most appropriate for the purpose of supporting the individual through the learning process with a view to promoting career development?

   A   Buddy

   B   Counsellor

   C   Mentor

   D   Instructor

                                                                                      (2 marks)

50   Gils is conducting an appraisal interview with his assistant Jill. He initially invites Jill to talk about the job, her aspirations, expectations and problems. He adopts a non-judgmental approach and offers suggestions and guidance.

   This is an example of which approach to performance appraisal?

   A   Tell and sell approach

   B   Tell and listen approach

   C   Problem solving approach

   D   360 degree approach

                                                                                      (2 marks)

Section 4

ANSWERS TO PILOT PAPER QUESTIONS

1   B

The span of control is concerned with the number of subordinates reporting directly to one person. The scalar chain concept relates to the number of levels in the management structure.

2   B

The basic principle that underlies marketing is that it is a management process that identifies and anticipates customer needs. The other distractors in the question refer to specific activities undertaken by a marketing function.

3   A

Successive reports on corporate governance (Cadbury, Higgs, etc.) have highlighted the increasingly prominent role that non-executive directors should take in large organisations. This has become an established best practice.

4   B

The task culture is appropriate where organisations can accommodate the flexibility required to adjust management and team structures to address the tasks that must be fulfilled. This is very common in large consultancy firms.

5   D

A situation analysis is carried out when deciding on strategic objectives. The organisation will have already decided on its mission statement and goals.

6   C

Greater accountability at lower levels will lead to greater empowerment of those taking decisions and hence greater motivation and commitment.

7   C

A manager is employed by the organisation and is therefore a constituent part of it. All the others are known as 'connected' stakeholders.

8   D

The organisation must constantly be aware of the needs of stakeholders with a high level of power and the ability to influence the organisation profoundly. Management decisions must therefore take most account of the needs of this group of stakeholders.

9   D

The primary aim of a public oversight board is to eliminate or minimise any actual or potential breaches of legislative requirements and to ensure compliance with regulations applicable to organisations within their terms of reference.

10   B

The ageing population trend is caused by a decreasing birth rate and a decreasing mortality rate.

11   D

An increase in public expenditure should increase the level of consumer demand and hence the level of economic activity. This would also be achieved by other measures, such as a reduction in taxation or a reduction in interest rates.

12   C

Frictional unemployment arises even when there are unfilled vacancies in the economy. It is because there is never a perfect match between the types of job available and their location with the skills of those seeking work and where they live.

13   B

Any environmental scan analyses the external factors that affect an organisation, often categorised as political, economic, social and technological factors.

14   B

Data protection legislation is formulated to protect the interests of data subjects who are private individuals. Not all data is regulated.

15   B

Diversity policies are intended to reduce recruitment and selection policies and processes that enable discrimination to arise on the basis of gender, race, lifestyle and age.

16   C

The components of effective demand in the economy are consumer spending, investment by enterprises, central and local government expenditure and the net gains from international trade.

17   A

Lobby groups are primarily established to influence political decision takers, such as the government and individual lawmakers.

18   C

Scientific management principles consider the ways in which the factors of production (land, labour, capital and the entrepreneurial function) can be combined to maximise efficiency in production. The founding principles are based on the work of Frederick Winslow Taylor.

19   B

The accounting function originated from the need to record transactions completely and accurately. Other requirements naturally evolved from this at a later stage.

20   A

Tax avoidance enables the individual or entity to apply legitimate rules to reduce the amount of tax payable. Tax evasion is always based on a deliberate intent not to pay tax that is lawfully due.

21   A

A transaction processing system enables all sales and purchase transactions to be recorded by volume and category.

22   B

The implementation of a budgetary control system would be the responsibility of the financial controller in many organisations. The internal auditor is not responsible for implementing systems, but is involved in monitoring the effectiveness of these systems.

23   C

Public utilities companies often have national or local monopolies and it is therefore necessary for their pricing structures to be subject to the scrutiny of a regulatory body.

24   B

An interest rate is the price of money. The output of the treasury function is directly affected by the price of funds to the organisation and the returns that can be made from surplus funds.

25   B

The IASB aims to promote consistency in corporate reporting by creating financial reporting standards to which major businesses are expected to adhere.

26   A

Payroll, purchase ledger and sales invoicing are core functions within the responsibility of the financial accountant.

27   A

Where price inflation is high, the value of money reduces consistently over time. Those who owe money (receivables) therefore pay back less capital in real terms, and interest rates seldom adjust adequately to compensate for this.

28   A

The internal auditor must have the right to report and is most accountable to the highest level of management (Directors) in the organisation. They must be free of influence from any individual manager, irrespective of seniority.

29   C

A computerised system can be costly to set up, though this disadvantage is essentially a short-term issue, as the running costs should offset this over time. A computer system should also reduce transaction processing time and the incidence of errors.

30   D

Systems audit is concerned with the effectiveness of the system itself and not the processes, activities or values of the organisation.

31   B

The external auditor has to ensure that the financial statements of the organisation truly reflect the activities of the business in the relevant accounting period. This assessment should be independent and therefore free from subjectivity on the part of the management of the client organisation.

32   A

Substantive tests verify the accuracy of the financial information.

33   A

Teeming and lading involves the theft of cash and is a type of fraud that is carried out by manipulating transactions. There would be most potential for this fraud within the sales department where cash may be received and remitted.

34   B

All control systems should be based on an assessment of areas of risk prior to the consideration of other factors.

35   B

The Ashridge model identifies four styles: autocratic; authoritarian; consultative; laissez-faire (or participative). The first of these is the least participative.

36   A

The Blake and Mouton managerial grid enables leadership styles to be categorised on a nine point scale with reference to concern for people and concern for production.

37   B

With the recent departures and the new staff joining the group, it will revert to the forming stage.

38   C

The words 'curious' and 'explore' confirm that the individual is a resource-investigator.

39   B

According to Herzberg, money is a hygiene factor (or dissatisfier). Although it is a powerful short-term motivator, it is questionable whether each individual increase in monetary reward will have a major long-term effect. According to Herzberg, 'A reward once given becomes a right'.

40   C

Consensus implies coming to decisions that are acceptable, paying due regard to the input of all members of the team.

41   B

Victor Vroom defines 'valence' as the individual's preference for a given outcome.

42   A

Handy's theory suggests that full-time, permanent workers are both expensive and inflexible in comparison with other elements of the shamrock. These other elements are part-time workers and independent contractors. A fourth leaf can be getting the customer to do the work.

43   D

The wheel facilitates transmission of the message directly to all receivers and therefore transmits most quickly.

44   B

Lateral communication is horizontal. Therefore, poor quality communication will result in poor coordination between team members.

45   A

Role playing exercises are most effectively used for skills development, including sales training. Other common business applications include effective selection interviewing and performance appraisal interviewing.

46   C

Product is the fourth component of the marketing mix. This term can also relate to a service as well as tangible products.

47   C

Competence testing evaluates and validates knowledge and the ability to apply these to given situations. It assesses whether the individual can actually do specified tasks.

48   B

A height restriction is a form of indirect discrimination on the grounds of gender. On average, men are taller than women.

49   C

A mentor has a longer-term role than buddies, counsellors or instructors.

50   B

The 'tell and listen' approach encourages input from the individual, promoting participation in the process by the appraisee.